Backdrop of the PakTurk Schools Crisis in Pakistan

The Ordeals of the Turkish Teachers

DREAMS INTERRUPTED

Engin Yiğit

DREAMS INTERRUPTED

**Backdrop of the PakTurk Schools Crisis in Pakistan
The Ordeals of the Turkish Teachers**

www.silencedturkey.org

Published: January, 2024
ISBN: 9798873911103

I dedicate this book foremost to the Kaçmaz and Ervan families and 108 Turkish educators and their family members who endured myriad hardships during the events in the wake of November 2016 PakTurk Schools crisis in Pakistan and survived notwithstanding the intense psychological violence and financial difficulties…

…and to our students, parents and truehearted friends who provided perpetual support and never abandoned us.

CONTENTS

Chapter 3: Faux Coup in Turkiye and Repercussions in Pakistan (July 15, 2016 - November 15, 2016)

Chapter 4: Tribulations in a Foreign Land (November 16, 2016 - September 27, 2017)

INTRODUCTION

It all started in 1995. What was sought to be materialized was perhaps a dream for many. Educators from Turkiye rolled up their sleeves to open schools in Pakistan and pleaded with philanthropic businesspeople who could support this project. Everyone believed this historic initiative and expansion would soon find its way into the Pakistani society. The meetings held with the Pakistani state officials to have the upcoming schools immediately open their doors to education in the sister country proved fruitful and auspicious. Without delay, the preparations for this historic project, a first in South Asia, were expedited and the school named PakTurk International College opened its doors to students in Islamabad in April 1995 with educators from Turkiye joined by their Pakistani counterparts. In a short time, the number of PakTurk Schools reached 28 across the country.

PakTurk Schools have carved themselves a niche among the most distinguished educational institutions in Pakistan, providing education to over 11.000 K-12 students across the country. These institutions, which also offered merit scholarships to bright and high-achieving students with limited financial means, impressed with their achievements in the national and international education and science competitions and represented Pakistan worldwide with pride and distinction, winning medals for the country in many disciplines.

While making a name for themselves in the country, PakTurk Schools also carried out numerous social projects. Thanks to its frequent charitable and humanitarian assistance drives, these educational institutions set their thrones in the hearts of millions across Pakistan. Especially in the wake of the natural disasters, PakTurk Schools stood by the affectees in their times of hardship and rendered selfless services with their teachers and students to alleviate pains and repair damages. To this end, the PakTurk educational institutions also drilled freshwater wells in several settlements with drinking water shortage and provided merit scholarships to high school and university students in need.

PakTurk institutions' educational achievements and humanitarian assistance activities throughout Pakistan earned the recognition of the Government of Pakistan. In June 2006, the President of the Islamic Republic of Pakistan conferred the PakTurk educational institutions the prestigious civil award Sitara-e-Eisaar (Star of Altruism) for their distinguished services.

Having snowballed from the last months of 2013 onwards, political developments in Turkiye inflicted a harsh impact on the state of affairs in Pakistan. Superficially felt throughout 2014, these developments evolved into repressive, lawless and violent practices in late 2015 and early 2016, especially with intelligence operations systematically deployed in November 2016 and onwards.

Between 2013 and 2019, the state-steered lawlessness for the persecution and oppression of the Turkish personnel of the PakTurk Schools, who worked devotedly alongside their Pakistani colleagues, reached incredible levels. As someone who closely observed the developments during this period and witnessed several wrongdoings, I consider it my duty to write about my observations and experiences.

This book comprises six chapters:

Chapter 1: Education System in Pakistan and the PakTurk Schools (1995-2013)

Chapter 2: Signal Flares of the Crisis (2013-2016)

Chapter 3: Faux Coup in Turkiye and Repercussions in Pakistan (July 15, 2016 - November 15, 2016)

Chapter 4: Tribulations in a Foreign Land (November 16, 2016 - September 27, 2017)

Chapter 5: Abduction of the Kaçmaz Family and the Aftermath (September 27, 2017 - July 4, 2018)

Chapter 6: Transfer of the PakTurk Schools to the Turkiye Maarif Foundation (September 15, 2017 - December 13, 2018)

The pressures applied on the PakTurk Schools, as you may have been familiar with from the media reports, and the persecution of the Turkish teachers will be discussed in this book, classified in a certain chronological order. After giving a brief information about the education system in Pakistan, the activities of the PakTurk Education Foundation will be emphasized.

Chapter 1

Education System in Pakistan
and the PakTurk Schools

(1995–2013)

EDUCATION SYSTEM IN PAKISTAN

Despite being a country with a deep-seated education tradition, Pakistan has not yet attained the desired quality and level of education due to its rapid population growth and the fact that most of the population live in rural areas and have limited opportunities.

Founded in 1947 under the leadership of '*Quaid-e-Azam*' (Great Leader) Muhammad Ali Jinnah, Pakistan is defined as the Islamic Republic of Pakistan in its 1973 Constitution, which is still in force. Majority of its 230 million population are Muslims. Hindus, Christians, and other religious minorities make up 10% of the population. The country's Islamic identity is also reflected in education. According to statistics, there are nearly 30,000 madrasas across the country. According to the data provided by several national and international media organizations, 1.5 to 3 million students study in these madrasas.

The number of madrasas registered a substantial rise after the founding of Pakistan. During the 11-year rule of General Zia-ul-Haq between 1977 and 1988, the number of madrasas increased dramatically. The steps taken by General Zia-ul-Haq to make Islamic ideology dominant in Pakistan are conspicuous.

Some researchers, who closely follow Erdogan's efforts to increase the number of similar schools (Imam-Hatip Schools) in Turkiye, ask the question "Is Erdogan the modern-day Zia-ul-Haq?" [See *"Turkiye Is Turning into the Next Pakistan"* by Eli Lake]

While most madrasas in Pakistan offer purely religious

education, a handful of madrasas offer courses in the applied and positive sciences. Madrasas disseminate the ideas of the schools and communities they belong to. In this context, thousands of students are educated in madrasas founded and run by prominent Islamic groups such as the Deobandis, Barelvis, Ahl al-Hadith, Ahl al-Bayt, and the Jamaat al-Islami. An issue debated both nationally and internationally for many years is who finances the existing madrasas. It is often reported that Saudi Arabia, Iran, and some Gulf countries are financing madrassas of certain schools of thought and hence managing the perception of Islam in Pakistan.

Apart from madrasas, public schools are insufficient to meet the country's educational needs. According to 2018 data, 63% of the population in Pakistan lives in rural areas. In Pakistan, a federation, the state could not invest adequately in rural areas due to budget distribution issues and miscellaneous provincial priorities. Poor children in rural areas move either to big cities or to nearby settlements with schools to receive education. Some families also send their children to boarding schools, which are not sufficient in number today. This places a financial burden on families with limited means.

As such, private schools fill the gaps in the country's education sector. Private schools account for 43% of the total education setup in the country. An issue that has been on the country's agenda lately and which politicians have had difficulty in responding to is the increase in private school fees at a rate inflicting the public with a massive financial burden. Consequently, families with strong financial means send their children to private schools while poorer families are forced to continue their children's education in public schools. This situation ignores the principle of equal opportunity in education and leads to the emergence of class conflict in society. This condition in Pakistan is not normal. Meanwhile, in Turkiye, private schools make up 1.5% of the entire education setup.

While the medium of instruction in private schools is mostly English, in most public schools it is Urdu. Up to high school, the national curriculum is followed generally. At high school level, the public-school students are prepared for the provincial education boards' Matriculation (SSC) and Intermediate (HSSC) examinations while the private school students prepare for the British IGCSE O and A Level Cambridge International Examinations.

Yet another important issue is the country's budget allocation for education remaining at 2-3%, which is financially insufficient to meet the infrastructure and needs of the education system. Unfortunately, the physical facilities of several public schools are not feasible in today's conditions.

Another issue requiring an urgent solution to improve the education in Pakistan is depriving girls of education. According to a Human Rights Watch report, 32% of school-age girls in Pakistan are out of school. Families influenced by the rhetoric of radical Islamic groups do not wish to have their daughters educated.

The world knew about Malala Yousafzai, the 2014 Nobel Peace Prize laureate from Pakistan, when Taliban militants – who had banned girls from attending school in the Swat Valley in northern Pakistan – gunned down her and her friends on their way to school. The fact that women in Pakistan are educated and have a voice of their own in society have disturbed some. Benazir Bhutto, a world-renowned politician and one of the few prominent Pakistani politicians who served as the Prime Minister, was assassinated in December 2007, five years before Malala was attacked.

FIRST PAKTURK SCHOOLS IN BUNGALOWS

Instead of large campuses that would take years to build at first, the pioneer Turkish educators who arrived in Pakistan with great ideals in the beginning of 1990s had launched their educational activities in bungalows repurposed as school buildings, a common practice in Pakistan, to primarily attune themselves with the country and its educational system.

The first school opened by the Turkish entrepreneurs through the official permission granted by the Federal Ministry of Education in Pakistan was the PakTurk Islamabad Boys College in April 1995. This school was followed by the PakTurk Islamabad Pre-School and Primary School in April 1997 and the PakTurk Karachi Pre-School and Primary School in August 1997.

Opening one after another, the PakTurk Schools spread across Pakistan in a short span of nine years, like seeds planted in fertile ground.

FROM BUNGALOWS
TO PURPOSE-BUILT CAMPUSES

Well-known and well-recognized in Pakistan, PakTurk Schools gained a new face with the campus schools from 2006 onwards, about 11 years after their founding. Especially after the October 2005 earthquake, which caused devastation in the Northwest Frontier Province and Azad Kashmir region, philanthropic Turkish businessmen and educators, who frequently visited Pakistan with aid organizations, contributed immensely to moving PakTurk Schools from bungalows to campuses.

The first campuses were built in Islamabad, Peshawar, Quetta, and Lahore. Afterward, the number of PakTurk Schools in campuses increased in these and other cities in Pakistan. The schools had the latest educational technologies and tools. Several guests who visited the schools were amazed by the physical conditions and modern laboratories and expressed their appreciation by saying that some of these facilities were not available even in universities.

The public demand for the PakTurk Schools increased as the physical conditions of the institutions improved, the quality of education and infrastructure increased, and dormitory facilities were provided to the students. By 2016, the number of students had reached 11,000.

As the academic and social achievements of the schools increased in leaps and bounds, the parents insisted to the school administrations to have this successful educational tradition crowned with an international university. This led to the implementation of solemn steps including the signing of protocols with the authorities and taking initiatives for the educational plot on which the univerrsity would be built. In 2012, after the official permissions, the project for the International Allama Iqbal University in Lahore was authorized and the wheels were set in motion for the realization of the project.

EDUCATION SYSTEM IN THE PAKTURK SCHOOLS

With its experienced, successful and devoted teaching staff, modern equipped schools and dynamic vision for a bright future, PakTurk educational institutions have become exemplary schools in Pakistan in a short time and have made a name for themselves.

With their staff specialized in preschool and elementary education from kindergarten to eighth grade in English-medium education, PakTurk Schools prepared high school students to Pakistan's local Matriculation (SSC) and Intermediate (HSSC) examinations besides the British IGCSE O and A Level Cambridge International Examinations, with their tradition of outstanding success.

Upholding their motto *"What is taught with love lasts forever"*, PakTurk Schools attached great importance to science and technology-based STEM education to ensure the participation of their students in national and international science and education competitions and maintain their quality of education at international standards.

Language education was also essential in PakTurk Schools. Besides an advanced level of English, Turkish was taught as well. Thanks to this, PakTurk Schools made a name for themselves in Turkiye and worldwide with their students who could sing Turkish songs and recite poems without an accent and mingle easily with the native speakers.

The nationwide Inter-School Mathematics Olympiad (ISMO) organized by the PakTurk Schools became a brand name in Pakistan. Ultimately, 12,000 students between grades

5 and 8 across the country participated in the competition. Annually, the highest-achieving grade 8 student was awarded the Al-Khwarizmi Prize in commemoration of Al-Khwarizmi, known as the father of mathematics. The award galas were as attractive as the Olympiads. The 2013 ISMO Award Ceremony was presided by Cemil Çiçek, then-Speaker of the Turkish Grand National Assembly, and his Pakistani counterpart Faisal Karim Kundi, then-Deputy Speaker of the National Assembly of Pakistan, with Turkish and Pakistani MPs. In 2016, Pakistan's Federal Minister of Education presided the last ISMO award ceremony.

PAKTURK SCHOOLS' ACHIEVEMENTS

PakTurk Schools had made a name for themselves and Pakistan in several local and international academic organizations. Competing on behalf of Pakistan in international science olympiads, the schools upheld the motto, *"It is all science, no fiction"* to emphasize their achievements.

As of 2015, PakTurk Schools had won 83 gold, 41 silver, and 70 bronze medals in local and international Olympiads, totaling 194 distinctive medals for Pakistan.

PakTurk Schools' achievements were not limited to the Olympiads; they were also lauded for their high university placement achievements in the national and Cambridge board examination systems. In 2015, PakTurk Lahore student Sania Nasir ranked first in the world in Cambridge International Examinations' A Level Accounting and first in Pakistan in A Level Economics, attaining success among millions of students worldwide.

Another field where the PakTurk students made a name for themselves was the Intel Science Olympiads. PakTurk students won the majority of the prizes in the Pakistan national rounds of the Olympiad and, as the country-level winners, successfully represented Pakistan in the international rounds held in the United States.

PakTurk Schools, making a name for themselves not only in sciences but also in humanities and arts, represented Pakistan with three students at the Model United Nations Diplomacy Conference held at the United Nations HQ in Geneva in 2016.

PAKTURK SCHOOLS RECEIVED PAKISTAN'S STATE AWARD

Since their inception in 1995, PakTurk Schools not only provided education but also fulfilled their social responsibility through humanitarian relief activities. PakTurk Schools were the first civil organization to reach the Azad Kashmir and the NWFP (now Khyber Pakhtunkhwa) provinces with their volunteer Turkish and Pakistani staff in the wake of the devastating October 2005 earthquake in northern Pakistan. Fulfilling the emergency humanitarian relief and rescue activities in the wake of the disaster, PakTurk teachers made great efforts to heal the wounds of the earthquake affectees.

The people of Turkiye were not insensitive to the resonance of the incident across the world, and they immediately extended their helping hand. Delivering much-needed humanitarian relief to the earthquake-affected localities in the NWFP and Azad Kashmir, *"Kimse Yok Mu Solidarity and Aid Association"* (KYM) built 10 fully-equipped schools in the region and handed them over to the state. PakTurk Schools provided local guidance and connected the KYM with the local authorities and the earthquake survivors.

In 2006, then-President Pervez Musharraf awarded Pakistan's distinguished civil service medal *Sitara-e-Eisaar* to the PakTurk teachers who had won the hearts of the Pakistani state and the people through their selfless efforts to ensure the precise delivery and distribution of the emergency humanitarian relief from Turkiye to the earthquake affectees. While conferring the *Sitara-e-Eisaar* to the PakTurk Schools' Director Fesih Çelik, President Musharraf said, *"Our nation will always remember you and your services."*

While the PakTurk Schools, which attained the favor of the state and the people, continued to expand their services across Pakistan, *Kimse Yok Mu Solidarity and Aid Association* opened a country office for effective streamlining of the humanitarian activities and addressing the emerging issues without delay.

BRIDGING HEARTS: KIMSE YOK MU SOLIDARITY AND AID ASSOCIATION

As an effective conduit for delivering the emergency humanitarian assistance from Turkiye to Pakistan in the wake of the 2005 Kashmir earthquake, *Kimse Yok Mu Solidarity and Aid Association* (KYM) opened a representative office to streamline its activities in Pakistan more effectively and regularly distributed humanitarian aid to people in hardship in various parts of the country. PakTurk Schools provided initial local guidance to the KYM for fulfilling emergency relief and reconstruction efforts in the flood-hit areas with an exclusive emphasis on rebuilding the educational and social infrastructure. With free cataract surgeries being a priority, the Association also built tube wells for people's access to clean water, provided the underprivileged with health services and social assistance, and so gained prominence among the social welfare organizations in Pakistan.

In the wake of the 2010 flood disaster in Pakistan, the people of Turkiye were once again mobilized to collect donations and extend a helping hand to the friendly country Pakistan. Having swiftly responded to the devastating disaster through its emergency relief activities, *Kimse Yok Mu Solidarity and Aid Association* channeled donations to the flood affectees in various locations. The Association built and delivered the Allama Iqbal Town, in Muzaffargarh, Punjab to the flood affectees in the region. Costing 4 million USD to build and consisting of 296 houses, a school, a mosque, 4 public parks, 10 shops, and a clean water tower, the Allama Iqbal Town was inaugurated and the flood-affectees were handed the keys and deeds of their newly-built houses in 2013 in a ceremony presided by Hamza Sharif, an MNA of the Punjab Assembly and the son of the then-Chief Minister of the Punjab province Mian Muhammad Shehbaz Sharif, Prime Minister of Pakistan as of July 2023. In addition to the *Kimse Yok Mu Solidarity and Aid Association* officials and philanthropists from Turkiye, members of the Punjab provincial assembly and the Turkish Grand National Assembly attended the event.

With its several projects and achievements, *Kimse Yok Mu Solidarity and Aid Association* was always with the people of Pakistan, rain or shine.

PAKTURK MERIT SCHOLARSHIPS

One of the prominent features that made PakTurk Schools popular and privileged and earned them the admiration of the public was the merit scholarships they distributed to the high-achieving students. Before the unwarranted intrusion in 2018, nearly 50% of PakTurk students were on scholarship.

Offering education and accommodation opportunities to successful students with no discrimination, the schools ensured that successful students lacking strong financial means had access to quality education.

PakTurk educational institutions' network of 28 schools included 3 government schools leased between 2001 and 2003 via protocols signed with the provincial ministries of education under the Government of Pakistan's "Adopt a School" program to revive underutilized or dilapidated government schools for education through partnership with private and non-governmental organizations. PakTurk Education Foundation modernized the physical infrastructure and educational facilities of these schools and inducted them into the high-achieving PakTurk Schools network. Among such schools were a K-5 school in the Islampura district of Lahore, a K-5 school in the Ali Chowk district of Multan, and a K-12 school in Khairpur Mirs in the Sindh province. Students in these schools were provided the same superior quality of education and training and the same care and affection as in the other 25 PakTurk schools in Pakistan.

Working in Multan, I frequently witnessed the happiness and gratitude of the parents and students of our Ali Chowk school for the educational activities and services provided by our Foundation. They were especially elated for their children who received a superior private school education by paying public school fees. When this government school first joined the PakTurk Schools in May 2003, it had only kindergarten and primary school classes. In time, our 5th grade students and their parents insisted us to start a middle and high school program because they wished to continue their education at the PakTurk Schools. Unfortunately, the unexpected political developments did not allow this to happen.

PakTurk Education Foundation provided perpetual educational support to their high-achieving students who wished to pursue university education in Pakistan or Turkiye through merit scholarships.

Our Pakistani colleagues would sometimes criticize us for the generosity of the scholarships, saying such long-term investments on students would not yield results. We kept assuring them saying the PakTurk students deserved scholarships notwithstanding their career plans and emphasized that the graduates would even return to their schools to teach like their Pakistani and Turkish teachers. In 2015, on the 20th anniversary of the PakTurk Schools, a substantial number of our graduates had become teachers at the PakTurk Schools and were lauded for their outstanding efforts. Witnessing the exquisite results of their efforts, our Pakistani colleagues were touched, and they perceived the prodigious benefit of trusting in the youth of their country and investing in the future through education.

PAKTURK SCHOOLS HEADLINED IN THE NEW YORK TIMES

On May 4, 2018, The New York Times ran a front-page article by Sabrina Tavernise with the headline *"PakTurk Schools Offer a Gentler Vision of Islam"*. In the wake of the 9/11 terrorist attacks, Pakistan suffered the repercussions of the rising radicalism and brand-new wars, especially in the Middle East and Afghanistan. Having lost tens of thousands of civilians and military personnel in the country's war against terrorism, Pakistan also kept struggling against the rampant anti-Western sentiments and radical tendencies in the underprivileged segments of the society due to the perpetual violence and conflicts in the region. PakTurk Schools' activities emphasizing universal human values over radical rhetoric and the model of education based on uplifting the youth with sublime morals and superior academic prowess did not escape the attention of The New York Times. In an impressive front-page article, the daily introduced its readers to the PakTurk Schools with their social activities and exemplary educational model against violence in the region. Journalists had interviewed the school administrators, teachers, and students and shared their observations during their visits to the schools. "While these schools alone may not be able to change the country, there is no doubt they are doing something to reduce the impact of radicalism in the region," Tavernise said in the article, which included interviews with the boarding students in the dormitories and various insights into the PakTurk Schools' model of education.

PAKISTANI STATE OFFICIALS CHOSE THE PAKTURK SCHOOLS FOR THEIR CHILDREN

High-ranking state officials too had their children and relatives educated in the PakTurk Schools. They interacted with and appreciated our institutions not only by hearsay, but also by experiencing the system of education and instructional quality very closely. For example, the children of the then-Federal Minister of Education, the children of a member of the National Assembly who later became the State Minister for Interior Affairs, and the grandson of Muhammad Yaqoob Khan, then-President of the Azad Kashmir, were among the students of the PakTurk School I managed in Islamabad.

As the chief guest of the Sports Week at our school, the President of the Azad Kashmir inaugurated the event where his grandson competed too. While appreciating the PakTurk School and their system of education, Muhammad Yaqub Khan expressed his pleasure to have made the right educational choice for his grandson at our school.

TURKISH STATE OFFICIALS PRAISED THE PAKTURK SCHOOLS

In the wake of the 2010 flash floods which especially devastated the Sindh province, Erdogan made an official visit to the flood-affected areas. He requested the Governor of Sindh Dr. Ishrat ul Ibad, who accompanied him during the visit, to allot the PakTurk Schools *"an educational plot in a convenient district of Karachi for the school building planned to be built there"*.

Similarly, during the same visit, former Mayor of Istanbul Kadir Topbaş too requested Mayor of Karachi Syed Mustafa Kamal to allot an educational plot for the campus school the PakTurk Schools planned to build in Karachi, adding: *"I vouch for the teachers and the administrators of these schools. They are exquisitely decent people. You can allot them a school plot with peace in mind. I also have my children educated in their schools."*

In 2006, Kayseri businessmen sponsored the PakTurk Boys' High School which was planned to be built in Islamabad and Mehmet Özhaseki, the Mayor of Kayseri Metropolitan Municipality, accompanied a delegation of 180 Kayseri businessmen and educators who came to the groundbreaking ceremony on a chartered plane. After the groundbreaking ceremony, the delegation attended a cultural program organized in their honor at the concert hall of the National Library of Pakistan, after which Mehmet Özhaseki took the stage and led a "himmet" (voluntary donation) meeting with the participation of Turkish and Pakistani businessmen to cover the construction and furnishing costs of the school. Amidst the astonished and admiring looks of the audience, the philanthropists from Kayseri committed to provide the expenses and materials for the construction and furnishing of the school in less than an hour. Within 8 months, a world-class school campus was built in Islamabad.

Syed Yusuf Raza Gilani, the then-Prime Minister of Pakistan, and the members of his cabinet welcomed the Turkish dignitaries and businessmen who had arrived in Pakistan for the groundbreaking ceremony of the Islamabad Boys' High School. The Prime Minister thanked them for the educational and social aid activities carried out by the

Turkish entrepreneurs and philanthropists. Mian Muhammad Shehbaz Sharif, Prime Minister of Pakistan as of July 2023, showed special interest in the PakTurk Schools and the Turkish educators in those days and insistently solicited their opinions on issues related to Turkiye as independent advisors, hosted the Turkish guests, whom he considered a forthcoming business potential, for dinner at his mansion in Lahore and treated them as VIP state guests during their stay in the city.

Turkish philanthropists and state officials such as Özhaseki, who witnessed and admired the care and special attention shown to the schools and their services by the Pakistani state officials, could not hide their surprise to express how prominently Turkiye was represented in Pakistan.

SHEHBAZ SHARIF'S REMARKS AT THE "IDEAL MAN AND IDEAL SOCIETY IN FETHULLAH GULEN'S THOUGHT" CONFERENCE IN NOVEMBER 2012

Mian Muhammad Shehbaz Sharif, then-Chief Minister of the Punjab, had insisted in May 2012 that the University of the Punjab in Lahore should expressly grant Fethullah Gulen an honorary doctorate as a token of appreciation for Gulen's contributions to the commendable development of Turkiye, especially in education and social fields. Sharif had also initiated the organization of the international conference "Ideal Human and Ideal Society in Fethullah Gulen's Thought" in November 2012. Speaking at the inaugural reception in honor of the national and international delegates attending the conference, Shehbaz Sharif addressed the audience with an indelible remark:

"When we look at today's Turkiye, we observe a rapidly developing and modernizing country. What is the factor behind this? Does Turkiye have oil, gas, or other significant minerals or natural resources? No, let me tell you, Turkiye has Fethullah Gulen. This added value bears more significance than any natural resources."

PRIME MINISTER NAWAZ SHARIF'S PRAISING REMARKS IN TURKIYE ON THE PAKTURK SCHOOLS

In 2014, Prime Minister Nawaz Sharif made an official visit to Turkiye to attend to the Turkiye-Pakistan-Afghanistan Tripartite Security Summit. "PakTurk Schools are doing an excellent job; they have a high standard of education. I had the chance to visit one school in Lahore," the Pakistani Prime Minister said in response to a question posed to him, adding "The schools strengthen the relations between the two countries."

Sharif's earnest statement sent a chill down the spine of the Turkish state officials, who – in the wake of the December 17/25, 2013 scandal – kept working overtime in their witch-hunt against the institutions and the participants of the Hizmet Movement across Turkiye and pressuring the Pakistani officials to close the schools in Pakistan. In Pakistan, Nawaz Sharif's words of praise were welcomed by the PakTurk officials amidst looming problems.

The third leader at the 2014 summit, Afghan President Hamid Karzai said of the Turkish schools in his country, "These schools provide a high-quality education for Afghan students, and we are very pleased to have them in our country."

PakTurk students at an event held at the Lahore Boys Campus

PakTurk Lahore Asifa Irfan Girls Campus

PakTurk Islamabad H-8 Girls Campus

PakTurk Islamabad Boys Campus

A PakTurk teacher with students

PakTurk students in a computer lab

PakTurk students in the school yard

*PakTurk students in a dance performance during
the Children's Day event*

PakTurk students in a classroom

Muhammad Yaqoob Khan, the then President of Azad Jammu and Kashmir, presenting a certificate to a PakTurk student

Principal Engin Yigit awarding a Gold Medalist Certificate to a student at the Sports Day

PakTurk students' remarkable National and International Accomplishments in 2015

PakTurk Schools are renowned for academic excellence, consistently producing high-achieving students in National and International Olympiads

Chapter 2

Signal Flares of the Crisis

(2013–2016)

Founded in 1995, PakTurk Schools have been a trusted brand recognized for the quality of their education and the local and international achievements of their students. In 2013, the Erdogan regime initiated a political and social crisis in Turkiye to cover its exposed massive corruption and graft network, and this affected the PakTurk Schools as well as the other educational institutions opened by the Turkish entrepreneurs around the world.

The polarizing and tense political environment created by the regime in Turkiye peaked with the Gezi Protests which started on May 28, 2013, in Istanbul. The government's harsh intervention against the innocent protests of the environmentalists demanding the protection of the trees in the Taksim district's Gezi Park escalated daily. With the disproportionate use of force by the police and the killing of 22 protesters within three months, the protests spread all over Turkiye, and a serious public backlash ensued against the Erdogan regime, leading even some members of his own party criticize his repressive policies.

PAKTURK MULTAN BOYS HIGH SCHOOL GROUNDBREAKING CEREMONY

On March 15, 2013, shortly before the Gezi protests, PakTurk educational institutions embarked on a new campus school project in Multan. Besides the Punjab Minister for Education and senior officials of the Punjab government, a contingency of five Turkish parliamentarians – mostly from Erdogan's party AKP – attended the groundbreaking ceremony of the school.

When asked by some journalists about the intimidation and oppression against the Hizmet Movement in Turkiye, Afif Demirkiran, AKP Deputy Chairman said, "This issue is exaggerated. The AKP has no intentional hostility against the Hizmet Movement." Meanwhile, while giving the Turkish parliamentarians a tour of the school plot, a female AKP deputy remarked, "I like the name of the Schools the most! What a beautiful name: Pak Turk, meaning in Turkish 'Pure Turk!'"

While the Gezi protests were still running hot, the corruption probes in Turkiye made the headlines like a blast on December 17, 2013. People everywhere talked about the police raids that revealed an expansive network of bribery and misappropriation involving Prime Minister Erdogan with his son Bilal besides some cabinet ministers and their sons. Erdogan made a harsh retort against the opposition who claimed his political life ended.

Curious, Erdogan was on an official visit to Pakistan when the anti-corruption police operations were launched in Turkiye. Almost immediately after receiving the news, Erdogan made a hasty retreat to Turkiye and claimed the corruption probes and operations were the parts of a dirty plan initiated by the Hizmet Movement through the police to slander him and his party. This way, he launched an extensive counterattack to cast aspersions upon the operations and the Hizmet Movement to save his political career, and even consolidate a longer rule. Under the negative light shone by Erdogan, the scapegoated Hizmet Movement and its volunteers were alleged as the cause of all evil and shady deeds against Erdogan and his party. A large segment of the public, even though they did not believe Erdogan's allegations against the Hizmet Movement, continued to support his politics, saying "Erdogan may be stealing from people, but he's working for the country."

HALTING THE MULTAN BOYS HIGH SCHOOL CONSTRUCTION

Shortly after its groundbreaking ceremony held with the participation of senior Turkish and Pakistani government officials, the construction of the school and its outbuildings was suspended in Multan by the provincial government. The school building was 70% complete with internal decoration and equipment installations pending. The educational equipment and supplies ordered from Turkiye for 700 students were ready to be installed. After a couple of days, the Punjab provincial government also unilaterally terminated the protocol of the school plot allocated to the PakTurk Education Foundation in Rawalpindi for a fee.

Having been notified of the suspension of the Multan school construction, PakTurk Education Foundation officials tried to make sense of the situation and kept making official attempts to revive and complete the construction of the school. An advisor to the Chief Minister of the Punjab province told the PakTurk Schools officials, "We brace so much pressure from Turkiye. We cannot suggest anything about your other schools, but we have stopped the construction of this one to alleviate the pressure. Please understand us and assist us throughout this process." Even though the official letter maintained the school construction was suspended for a certain duration, the steps taken to restart the construction yielded no results, unfortunately.

On November 16, 2016, the crisis of PakTurk educational institutions peaked with the Government of Pakistan's sudden decision to deport the Turkish teachers working in the PakTurk Schools. This was prompted by several decisions, including the suspension of the construction of the Multan Boys' High School, the unilateral termination of the protocol for the school plot in Rawalpindi, and the unilateral termination of the protocol for the university plot allocated to the PakTurk Education Foundation in Lahore.

The process, which started with the major anti-corruption operations in Turkiye coinciding with Erdogan's visit to Pakistan on December 23-24 and Erdogan's direct pressure upon Pakistan to close the PakTurk Schools, kept on with a steady momentum of escalation.

REVOCATION OF THE UNIVERSITY PERMIT

Soon after the abovementioned suspension of the school construction, the Punjab provincial government announced its unilateral cancellation of the protocol for the International Allama Iqbal University with the PakTurk Education Foundation, notwithstanding all groundworks. The land allocated to the university was immediately taken back by the Punjab government officials.

In the wake of the successive suspension and cancellation decisions, the officials of the PakTurk Schools were solemnly concerned about how things would turn out soon. With these developments in progress, the Turkish Ambassador in

Islamabad was reported in national and social media to have intensified his visits to the government officials in Islamabad to consolidate the Turkish regime's pressure on the Pakistani government to close the PakTurk Schools.

NON-EXTENSION OF VISAS AND RESIDENCE PERMITS

Notwithstanding the consecutive problems faced by the PakTurk educational institutions, there was still hope that no serious problems would occur having visas and residence permits extended. No one wanted to even think a problem would surface about visa extensions especially when PakTurk schools were well known to the Pakistani authorities for more than 20 years and its services to the people of Pakistan were appreciated by the state officials. While the paperwork for routine visa extension and residency procedures was in progress, some were still worried about imminent snags. For PakTurk employees whose visas and residence permits were to expire in September 2016, the required documents for extension were submitted to the relevant department of the Ministry of Interior of Pakistan in April of the same year.

The authorities received the documents. In time, whenever asked on each follow-up visit, they always replied "The procedure is in progress, don't worry". In the previous cases, the visas of the Turkish educators at the PakTurk Schools had been extended for two years as a kind gesture. The change in attitude during the last application made PakTurk officials wonder what had gone wrong. It later turned out that the Turkish educators' visa cases had not been processed in the following months either. We learned albeit so late that the officials stalled us until the time was right.

JULY 15 COUP STAGE PLAY

We kept following with full curiosity the developments in Pakistan and Turkiye, and like everyone else, we kept worrying for the future of the Hizmet Movement and our schools in Pakistan.

Come July 15, 2016, and we were appalled by the news of the so-called coup attempt. We were glued on television and computer screens to learn more details of the infamous uprising and the immediate tragedies it left in its wake. On that bloody and treasonous night, Erdogan blamed the Hizmet Movement right from the very start of the incident and, with no evidence, alleged that Fethullah Gulen was behind the coup. Over seven years after the coup attempt, and although Erdogan and his partisans run the country in a totalitarian manner, they still could not show any official evidence to support this claim.

In Pakistan, the Turkish Embassy in Islamabad and the Turkish Islamists' political allies across the country took advantage of the situation and spread the word through social media and other media outlets alleging that the PakTurk Schools were linked to the coup attempt in Turkiye to distort the public opinion in Pakistan. The grandson of the late leader of Pakistan's leading Islamic party and several other political Islamists or pro-Ottoman Caliphate social media users invited locals to stage protests in front of PakTurk school buildings. Former Prime Minister Imran Khan, an avid social media personality and the leader of the 'most promising' opposition party back then, reacted to such radical rhetoric circulated on Twitter by asking, "What could Pakistani students studying in PakTurk Schools in Pakistan, five thousand kilometers away from Turkiye, have to do with the coup there?"

Due to increasing threats by the social media trolls targeting the PakTurk Schools on social media in Pakistan, the school administrators contacted the local law enforcement officials to take precautions. They expressed their solemn concerns and demanded immediate measures to prevent any negative incident. The smear campaign supervised by the Turkish Embassy in Islamabad on social media and national media outlets could thus be deflected and, thankfully, the first stage of the crisis was overcome without any unpleasant incident.

Targeting the Hizmet Movement worldwide on the pretext of the coup, the Erdogan regime mounted exclusive pressure on Pakistan. Faced with the multifaceted pressure to close the schools, local and international media in Pakistan showed closer interest in the schools. The million-dollar question was, "Will 28 PakTurk schools with 11,000 students be closed down?"

Reporters from media organizations and agencies such as the BBC World, Reuters, Voice of America, The New York Times, Washington Post, AP, and AFP, besides the members of Pakistan's national visual and print media, kept requesting interviews from the head office of our schools. Modestly dealing with all media organizations on behalf of the PakTurk institutions, I would also spend the longest days of my life. Every visiting media organization wished to know the headline matter of their news report: "Will PakTurk Schools be closed down under Erdogan's pressure?"

During weeks of media coverage and tense atmosphere, PakTurk Schools' most loyal friends were the parents, who stood for the institutions by all means by providing personal and moral support. Press conferences held by the Parents and Teachers Association (PTA) members attracted huge interest in the media. Consecutive news reports conveyed the PakTurk parents' views that the PakTurk Schools should continue undeterred and recommended the Government of Pakistan not to sacrifice the PakTurk Schools to stoke the internal politics of another country.

PESTERING VISITS TO THE
PAKTURK SCHOOLS IN ISLAMABAD

The municipal officers from the Capital Development Authority (CDA) in Islamabad, who had been visiting the schools on a normal schedule until then, started to inspect schools intensively in the wake of the July 2016 coup conspiracy. They threatened the schools with potential fines if the missing components (!) were not completed. PakTurk Schools had an infrastructure and education standard far ahead of most private schools in Pakistan, let alone public schools. The officials started to pinpoint and report simple issues as major problems. This accelerated exerting pressure on the institutions through the local authorities.

Considering the recommendations of the local authorities, our educational institutions immediately implemented the requested changes without any reaction and showed utmost care to cooperate with the officials. When a PakTurk official visited the Capital Development Authority, some officials told him about the rumor circulated by senior officials that the "PakTurk Schools would be seized in August 2016". As the saying goes, "Bad news travels fast", from those days onwards, almost everyone who visited the schools reckoned "what consequences the turmoil could bring, and how they could benefit from it all."

TURKISH AMBASSADOR LAUNCHED ANTI-PAKTURK CAMPAIGN

The then-Turkish Ambassador in Islamabad Sadık Babür Girgin augmented his active smear campaign against the Pak Turk Schools. Within the frame of his official attempts to have the schools closed, he visited the local authorities in the cities and provinces where the schools were located and held negotiations over the institutions. The details of these visits with dark plots were occasionally reported in Pakistan's national media and voiced by senior officials who visited the schools.

The Ambassador, who tried to impress the guests with such unpleasant statements during the special events he organized at the Embassy, quipped to some Pakistani private school owners and the leaders and members of political Islamist groups whom he deemed his friends that the PakTurk Schools would soon be seized and be handed to them. In this vein, the owner of an elite private school chain in the country, who always considered the PakTurk Schools a tough competitor, unexpectedly came to visit my school, which had the most attractive building and educational equipment, and wanted to have a tour, although he had never paid a visit before and had never wanted to be seen with us under normal circumstances. The reason for his visit was later revealed to be a follow-up of his meetings with the Turkish Ambassador in Islamabad and the promises he had been given.

After the July 15 bloody coup plot, the Ambassador held a press conference with a cherry-picked media attendance at the Turkish Embassy building and declared that "the PakTurk schools were linked to the coup attempt and should be closed down." The Ambassador's statements targeting the PakTurk Schools found a sounding board in the national media and saw heavy rotation, making the PakTurk Schools once again the center of attention in the public opinion.

In my personal meetings with several journalists who frequented my school, none asked me the question "Have you, or your institutions, been involved in a coup?" Considering that almost half a century of Pakistan's 76-year history is no stranger to military interventions and coups, it can be understood that everyone in the country knows so well what a coup looks like and how it is carried out. In an interview with the BBC Urdu correspondent Irum Abbasi at our school, I asked her, "If there was a coup in Pakistan, would anyone take to the streets to protest?" and she replied, "No, absolutely not, it's too dangerous!" Constructive thinkers in Pakistan, well aware of the features of the coup in Turkiye and the postmodern way it was carried out, did not even think that a transnational civil society movement, especially a community engaged in mainstream educational, business, media, and sociocultural activities, could be part of such a dastardly attempt. General Pervez Musharraf, once the most powerful figure in Pakistan, spent a significant part of his childhood in Turkiye during his father's posting to the Embassy of Pakistan in Ankara and received education in Turkiye until 1956 when he turned 13, and came to power in October 1999 through a coup d'état. Knowing the military prowess of the Turkish Armed Forces, all Pakistanis I met unanimously said that if a well-equipped army staged a coup, it would be out of the question for the people to prevent it.

TURKISH OFFICIALS' VISITS TO PAKISTAN

Starting from the end of 2013, not only Prime Minister Erdogan but also senior officials from the Turkish Ministry of Foreign Affairs, Directorate of the Religious Affairs, and several other Turkish public institutions visited Pakistan regularly to hold negotiations and pressure the Pakistani authorities to close the PakTurk Schools. Between 2014 and 2017, Erdogan made four annual official visits to Pakistan without fail. Each time he visited, he denigrated the PakTurk Schools to his counterparts and made attempts to have the schools closed. Soon, these attempts evolved into constant demands to have the PakTurk Schools transferred to the Erdogan-regime backed Turkiye Maarif Foundation (TMF). On November 16, 2016, leaving for Pakistan from Turkiye, he expressed his satisfaction with the Pakistani government's "gesture" of deporting Turkish teachers from the country, even though he had not got what he really wanted. Pakistani authorities had still not yielded to his intense demands to have the PakTurk Schools transferred to the Turkiye Maarif Foundation (TMF); they feared a public backlash if they had transferred the schools to the TMF in tandem with the deportation of the Turkish educators from Pakistan.

On August 2, 2016, an incident made waves in the Pakistani media. The then-Turkish Foreign Minister Mevlüt Çavuşoğlu paid an official visit to Pakistan. The tensions were visible right from the beginning of the visit. During the press conference with his Pakistani counterpart, the media asked the then-Advisor to the Prime Minister in Foreign Affairs Sartaj Aziz, "Will you close the PakTurk Schools?" to which Aziz replied, "There is no question of closing the schools, but we are working on alternatives so the education of the students must not be disrupted." In this press conference broadcast live by Pakistan's state television PTV besides several private TV networks, Mevlüt Çavuşoğlu's coarse attitude towards his Pakistani counterpart and the remarks he made after hearing the answer that the PakTurk Schools would not be closed were palpable to the eyes and ears.

Dr. Mehmet Görmez, the then-President of the Directorate of the Religious Affairs, who was deployed as a puppet by the Erdogan regime to undermine the credibility of the Hizmet Movement in Pakistan and elsewhere on "religious grounds", also visited Pakistan. He slandered the schools and their Turkish staff to his Pakistani counterparts and opinion leaders through allegations that would astonish even the devil himself. He defamed the PakTurk Schools and the Turkish educators and made propaganda against the institutions.

Adopting a full-court press in exerting pressure on the Pakistani officials, Erdogan's AKP did its best to keep these visits uninterrupted. On March 2, 2017, the then-Chief of General Staff Gen. Hulusi Akar was sent to Pakistan to demand the transfer of the PakTurk Schools under the pretext of bilateral defense agreements.

Following these developments, the PakTurk Education Foundation took the matter to court. The judge summoned officials from the Ministry of Interior and the Ministry of Education and asked for an explanation about transferring PakTurk Schools and the related media reports. Officials from both ministries told the judge there was no agenda for transferring the schools and that the news reports did not reflect the truth.

PAKISTANI OFFICIALS' VISITS TO TURKIYE

Holding sway over Pakistan and the largest province Punjab, Mian Muhammad Nawaz Sharif and Mian Muhammad Shehbaz Sharif had cordial links with Prime Minister Erdogan that went beyond the official rapport. In the wake of the July 2016 coup attempt, the frequency of invitations extended from Turkiye to Pakistani government officials increased and the officials could attend almost every prominent international event hosted by the Erdogan regime.

Then the Chief Minister of the Punjab and now the Prime Minister of Pakistan as of July 2023, Shehbaz Sharif took to attending all invitations he received from Erdogan with great enthusiasm. The two discussed their business alongside a bilateral national agenda and made mutual promises. If the rumors circulating in the Pakistani media were to be trusted, Shehbaz Sharif had substantial investments in Turkiye, especially in real estate.

After the July 15 coup conspiracy, a group of parliamentarians and senior bureaucrats from Pakistan visited Turkiye "to express solidarity with the Turkish government and offer condolences for the lost lives". During the reception held at the Presidential Palace in Ankara, the AKP's fabricated discourses and allegations over the coup were reiterated with the highlight demanding the immediate closure of the PakTurk Schools in Pakistan.

While Pakistani government officials kept visiting Turkiye with unprecedented frequency, it was reported in the Pakistani media that Imran Khan, the cricketer turned opposition figure showcased as the leader to oust the Sharif brothers from power in the 2018 general elections, preferred Turkiye as a meeting place with his children arriving from the UK.

Notwithstanding its fading interest in sustaining the Sharif government, Pakistan's military, including the Chief of General Staff and the Chief of Army Staff, paid high-level visits to Turkiye as well. In addition to these, the then-Chief Justice of the Supreme Court of Pakistan visited Turkiye and held a tête-à-tête with Erdogan in Ankara.

INTRIGUES THROUGH THE OIC

On October 17, 2016, the Organization of Islamic Cooperation Foreign Ministers Meeting was held in Tashkent, Uzbekistan. During the sessions, Turkiye upheld its demand for having the Hizmet Movement proscribed as a terrorist organization by all member countries. Despite no official resolution was made to this end, the pro-Erdogan media in Turkiye reported the event as if an official resolution was unanimously passed by the Organization of Islamic Cooperation and unconditionally adopted by the participating countries. Despite the absence of such a statement in the official declaration issued after the meeting, the Turkish authorities conducted the usual perception management and circulated the fake news in both national and international media as if all OIC-member countries accepted the AKP's falsehood and declared the Hizmet Movement a so-called 'terrorist' organization.

During a chat at a civil society organization in late October 2016, a Pakistani official of the Ministry of Foreign Affairs who attended the OIC summit said the Pakistani delegation were surprised by the hasty and unfocused behavior of the Turkish delegation and the Turkish Foreign Minister at the OIC meeting, highlighting that the Turkish delegation had left the room after having their agenda noted and re-entered the conference hall sometime later when the deliberations on Kashmir had been over. The official said the Turkish delegation later asked, "When are we discussing Kashmir?", revealing "the pitiable extent of significance they attached to the other agenda of the summit". He was surprised to see the Turkish delegation posting so-called "OIC resolutions" on social media despite the OIC meeting concluded without accepting Turkiye's proposition and passing no special resolution on proscribing the Hizmet Movement.

Pakistan, a member of the Organization of Islamic Cooperation, was later lured to a tight spot by the manipulative discourse of the Turkish Foreign Ministry which exploited the OIC meeting and resolutions for its own schemes.

PakTurk Education Foundation's management in

Islamabad was increasingly concerned about the Turkish Embassy's persistent efforts to headline the PakTurk Schools issue in the national press. What was feared happened: The Turkish Ambassador in Islamabad issued and circulated statements and letters across Pakistan, manipulating the declaration of the Organization of Islamic Cooperation.

In time, the Embassy presented this falsehood to the courts in all cases it was involved. Using this fiction as evidence, the Ambassador demanded the handover of the PakTurk Schools to the Turkish government and the arrest and extradition of the Turkish educators to Turkiye.

PAKISTAN GOVERNMENT SUED KARADENIZ ELEKTRIK (KARKEY)

A subsidiary of the Karadeniz Holding, the Karkey Karadeniz Elektrik Uretim (KKEU) was one of the 12 rental power companies awarded contracts by Asif Ali Zardari's PPP government between 2008 and 2009 to resolve the power crisis plaguing Pakistan for the last many years.

In April 2011, a Karkey power ship docked at the Karachi port to supply electricity to the national grid as per the agreement. The company failed to generate 231 megawatts as required under the agreement, even though the Government of Pakistan had made an advance payment of $9 million as capacity charges. Having seen that the floating power plant could produce between 30 and 55 megawatts at an exorbitant cost of Rs41 (Pakistani rupees) per unit against the contract, Pakistan suffered a 50 per cent increase in the refund claim between $80 million and $120 million. While the Government of Pakistan ceased receiving services from the Karkey, revoked the contract unilaterally, and did not allow the power ship to leave the Karachi port until the conflict was resolved, the National Accountability Bureau (NAB) filed a reference against the Karkey Karadeniz Elektrik Uretim (KKEU). The Turkish company requested a plea-bargain deal saying it was ready to pay $18 million to the NAB with a promise that it would not go for international arbitration if the offer would be accepted by the Government of Pakistan.

Some politicians moved the Supreme Court of Pakistan and the then-Chief Justice Iftikhar Mohammad Chaudhry insisted the Government of Pakistan to recover Pakistan's total loss of $120 million from the Karkey. The Turkish company responded by moving the International Centre for Settlement of Investment Disputes (ICSID) under the World Bank and sought compensation for the direct and indirect losses and the wear-and-tear suffered by its power ship which remained impounded at the Karachi port for nearly 16 months.

The forgotten court case in Pakistan was followed and won by the Karkey Karadeniz Elektrik in 2017. Even though the Government of Pakistan claimed the ICSID and the Karkey were bound by a non-disclosure agreement and would finalize a settlement amount, the news reports in Pakistan during September 2017 stated Karkey's demand from the Government of Pakistan as approximately 1.2 billion dollars, including the $800 million compensation award with interest decreed by the International Centre for Settlement of Investment Disputes (ICSID).

Pakistani media reported the national economy would receive a serious blow if the government chose to pay such an exorbitant amount in lump sum. It was also reported on social media that then-Prime Minister Nawaz Sharif urged his brother Shehbaz Sharif, then the Chief Minister of the Punjab Province, to meet Erdogan and request his arbitration between the Government of Pakistan and the Karkey Karadeniz Elektrik.

Pakistan's dire straits bestowed Erdogan a worthwhile trump card. It turned out that the prospective waiver of the compensation award by the Karkey Karadeniz Elektrik could be a key bargaining chip for transferring the PakTurk Schools to the Turkiye Maarif Foundation (TMF). In time, it would be revealed that the Pakistani authorities and the Erdogan regime had agreed to gradually materialize the scheme of seizing control of the PakTurk Schools. The government order for the expulsion of the Turkish teachers from Pakistan and the Supreme Court of Pakistan's lightspeed verdict on transferring the PakTurk Schools to the TMF hinted at the milestones of this scheme.

PAKISTAN AND THE ISOLATED STATES WORLDWIDE

Increasingly in the global spotlight since the early 1980s due to regional conflicts and political or religious debates, Pakistan had been termed an isolated state by the beginning of the 21st century. Despite its key geographical location and key role in ending the Cold War, Pakistan was shown in a negative light for the radical elements that plagued the society especially after the Soviet invasion of Afghanistan. Some analysts went the distance to define Pakistan as a "friendless" country, mentioning its "volatile" foreign policy based on its strategic partnerships with countries like China and the United States, besides its religious and cultural ties with Turkiye, Iran and Saudi Arabia.

Known as Central Asia's gateway to the warm seas, Pakistan has been in tense relations with India to the east, at odds with war-torn Afghanistan to the north, and cautious about its western neighbor Iran for sectarian reasons.

"Alone" in the world, Pakistan has three countries it could call "friends": China, Saudi Arabia and Turkiye. Except for China, none of these are Pakistan's neighbors, and Malaysia has recently joined the bloc for economic benefits. With the Saudis providing Pakistan with financial support, expatriate employment, and emergency oil, and Pakistani soldiers taking an active part in the protection of the Saudi Royal Family, Pakistan was compelled to keep safe distance from Iran, which was considered an enemy state by the Saudi regime.

During the Russo-Afghan War, Western countries defined Pakistan as a "non-NATO member allied country" and a large contingency of aid and logistics to Afghanistan were channeled through Pakistan. Despite these, some Western countries alleged Pakistan played both sides, did not take adequate measures against radical elements in the country, and turned a blind eye to such elements shuttling between Afghanistan and Pakistan during the conflicts and sheltering in porous and mountainous border regions. The last straw was the "revelation" that Usama bin Laden had been living for years in the outskirts of Abbottabad, a garrison city 135 kilometers from the capital Islamabad, while the Pakistani authorities had taken no action against him.

As such, while it could not get due attention and respect from the Western world and was sort of isolated for various reasons, Pakistan cherished its "three friends" more on each day. Hence, as mentioned several times by several officials, Pakistan ventured to please and placate Turkiye by following a positive stance towards every request from Turkiye, rain or shine.

Meanwhile, Turkiye-Pakistan relations go back to the Ottoman period. The Muslims of the South Asia, and especially in the subcontinent, were not indifferent to the social and economic hardships of the Ottoman Empire, which fought against several world powers in several fronts extending from Europe to Hejaz before and during the World War I. An oft-narrated convention of Muslims in Lahore at the beginning of the 20th century with the participation of Allama Dr. Muhammad Iqbal, the spiritual founder and national poet of Pakistan, sheds light on the profundity of the South Asian Muslims' interest in and devotion to the people of Anatolia, today's Turkiye.

Allama Iqbal took the podium and delivered a powerful speech that stirred the emotions of the congregation. In his address, he said the heartland of the Ottoman Caliphate needed urgent assistance and that the Muslims of the subcontinent should reach out to their brothers and sisters in faith immediately. The Muslims of the subcontinent, the ancestors of today's Pakistan, extended a much-needed helping hand to the people in Anatolia that day by donating while they themselves were in dire need. This and successive aids could only reach Turkiye at the beginning of the Republican era. When Turkiye solemnly needed emergency help, the sensitivity of the prospective people of Pakistan elated the people of Turkiye beyond expression. Years later, when Pakistan needed help in times of disaster and calamity, the people of Turkiye stood by their Pakistani brothers and sisters the same way and reciprocated the historical friendship at every opportunity.

Cooperation between peoples has been a manifestation of love and affection and was based on friendship from time immemorial. The heartfelt and unconditional reception meted out to the PakTurk Schools in Pakistan can be appraised from this aspect.

Once I asked a Pakistani diplomat from the Ministry of Foreign Affairs, "What makes Pakistan so subtle and particular in its relations with Turkiye?" and he replied, "Pakistan is a politically isolated country, and we cannot afford to commit mistakes against any brotherly country and government supporting us. Or else, we may be impaired. We must establish close relations with all Turkish governments to be sure of any adverse rejoinder from them."

PakTurk Schools got their share from the consequences of the Pakistani visits of the officials who shuttled between 'alone' Pakistan and Turkiye, which did not hesitate to exploit the circumstances situation for its own interests. Pakistani officials eventually bowed to the pressure of the AKP administration.

ECONOMY IN PAKISTAN

For several years, Pakistan has been struggling with myriad problems in education to social justice, from social justice to economy. Pakistan allocates a large part of its budget to defense due to tensions with neighbors, rendering the Pakistan Armed Forces as the most powerful institution for the country's defense and, occasionally, politics.

Power generation gap and distribution losses have been a crippling problem across the country while it tries to step on industrialization efforts and shape the economy as per the dynamic changes. Even in the capital Islamabad, one may experience power cuts for 7 to 12 hours a day during power crises. In smaller cities, this may last up to 18 hours. A Pakistani colleague once joked, "Despite the power issue in our country, we have succeeded in electrifying our toddlers' first words. They no longer start by mere 'Mom' or 'Dad'. They keep hearing us talking about the electricity and, skipping many words, start talking by forming basic sentences like, *'bhijli wapas aa gai'* (electricity is back) or *'bhijli chale gaya'* (electricity is gone).

Despite its great potential, Pakistan is fragile in economy while plagued with snags in the supply and distribution of electricity, an indispensable resource for industries and residences.

In Karachi, Pakistan's largest city, thefts and armed robberies are commonplace while one may often witness the mob roaming the streets, terrorizing the public. Frequent disruptions in municipal services to some districts result in garbage heaps and water shortages, troubling the residents.

Instead of finding lasting solutions to the country's problems, politicians in general have become adept at diverting attention by using social polarization to augment political gains. While civilian governments oscillate between two or three main parties, politicians spread the solution of festering problems over a long period.

Sadly, corruption has been a common discussion in Pakistan and is said to have almost taken over the state for a period. Former President of Pakistan Asif Ali Zardari, the husband of the late Prime Minister Benazir Bhutto, who served between 1988 and 1990 and 1993 and 1996, was implicated in corruption and was dubbed "Mr. Ten Percent" for allegedly carving 10% perks from every business that passed his desk. In addition to Asif Ali Zardari, who was the President while his party PPP was the government between 2008 and 2013, the Sharif family, initiated into active politics by former President General Zia-ul-Haq and has been in and out of power in Pakistan as the leaders of the PML-N since the late 1980s, has also been implicated in corruption. Due to these corruption cases, former Prime Minister Nawaz Sharif was arrested and imprisoned in 2018. Sharif, who was released conditionally due to health problems, did not return from the UK where he had gone for treatment. His daughter, Maryam Nawaz, who has been rumored to lead the party after her father, was found guilty in the same case and was jailed for some time.

In April-May 2023, former cricketer and the leader of Pakistan Tehreek-e-Insaaf (PTI) Imran Khan, who served as the Prime Minister between 2018 and 2022, was implicated in a National Accountability Bureau inquiry along with his wife Bushra Bibi and other PTI leaders on allegations of a settlement between the PTI government and a Pakistani property tycoon, which reportedly incurred a loss of £190 million pounds (around 68 billion Pak rupees in May 2023) to the national treasury. According to the charges, Imran Khan and other accused allegedly misappropriated the £190 million pounds recovered by the UK National Crime Agency (NCA) from the Pakistani property tycoon and deposited into a bank account opened by the Supreme Court of Pakistan in adjustment of the property tycoon's fine to be defrayed to the national treasury. Imran Khan and the other accused are alleged to have channeled this amount into a personal account and received unwarranted gain in connivance with the property tycoon, alleged to have provided Khan, in return of the amount reimbursed from the UK, over 53 acres of land in a district of the Punjab province for a private university named Al Qadir University.

The country's economic and political situation plays into the hands of foreign countries, some of which can dictate their wishes through the debt and aid they provide to Pakistan. Saudi Arabia's aid has placed Pakistan, a prominently Sunni country, under the influence of the Salafist movements. It is credibly reported that millions of children study in madrassas affected by the Salafi tradition.

Knowing the circumstances in Pakistan, the Erdogan regime untied the strings of its black budget purse, so to speak, to get what it wished from Pakistan through a transactional foreign policy. At a junction when the financial crisis in Pakistan deepened, the Governor of the State Bank of Pakistan visited Turkiye and agreements were signed for direct money transfers between the two countries. The way Erdogan waived in 2019 – with a single presidential touch of a pen, so to say – the billion-dollar compensation the Karkey

Karadeniz Elektrik would otherwise receive from Pakistan sheds an assorted light on the post-July 2016 transactional relations between the two countries.

Although Turkiye reiterated its promise to provide financial aid to Pakistan under all circumstances, it was widely known that its prominent objective was to have the PakTurk Schools transferred to the Maarif Foundation. Almost every issue discussed between the countries was conditional on the schools changing hands. In the Free Trade Agreement awaited to be signed between the two countries for over seven years, the Pakistani interlocutors were kept waiting as Turkiye hinted no action would be taken until the transfer of the PakTurk Schools was finalized.

USURPED INSTITUTIONS UNDER THE GUISE OF 'POST-JULY 15' DAMAGE CONTROL

AKP blamed the Hizmet Movement after the treacherous coup conspiracy and closed and confiscated all its institutions in Turkiye. Lending their influence over masses to the Erdogan regime across Turkiye, politically-opinionated Muslim religious leaders launched unprincipled and immoral attacks against their 'brothers and sisters in Islam' and declared everything and everybody affiliated with the Hizmet Movement as war spoils. Such religious (!) leaders kept issuing fatwas it was *halal* and commendable to seize the assets of the Hizmet Movement, and unashamedly appeared in political rallies to slander the participants of the Hizmet Movement with unspeakable insults, including legitimizing to keep the 'wives and children of the Hizmet participants as slaves' in their war against the Movement. Intoxicated by their ego and the in-trend Islam-mongering *politics*, they asserted all was fair in war(!).

While the Erdogan regime kept slandering innocent people as terrorists, it also implemented its scheme to compel thousands of people to starvation by dismissing them from the civil service. Managing perceptions to deny employment in the private sector and restoration of basic citizenship rights to those they blacklisted, the AKP officials upheld treachery and illegitimacy as their code of conduct to yield the best benefits from the aftermath of the July 15, 2016 debacle they engineered for consolidating their political ambitions and illicit wealth. They kept seeking fresh ways to lay their hands on the private educational institutions and businesses owned and operated by the Hizmet-inspired people and companies in and out of Turkiye and exploit them in collaboration with their like-minded Islam-monger communities and organizations at home and abroad.

It is no secret that various religious communities in Pakistan were and have been approached by the AKP through lucrative offers. While it is yet to be known what was promised to whom or who and how much was given, it has been revealed the Erdogan regime took crucial steps in this direction. A late Pakistani businessman with an intensive political Islamist background, who befriended the Hizmet volunteers for several years in Lahore, asked us for a "friendly advice" saying, "The officials in Turkiye promised to transfer the Fatih University to my organization for free. What would you suggest about this?" We told him about the legal status of these institutions and the way they had been usurped by the incumbent regime through unsubstantiated claims would certainly come up in the future. We also told him that the Erdogan regime kept committing flagrant crimes and wished to make likeminded entities and people like him partners in their crimes merely for financial reasons. Hearing these, he said he would refuse the offer.

The Erdogan regime resorted to assorted intrigues and illegalities, especially using the state apparatus and black budget as a leverage to compel the Pakistani authorities to have the PakTurk Schools transferred to the Maarif Foundation and have the Turkish educators expelled from Pakistan. Taking pride in their transgression, the Turkish officials did not hold back from constantly pressuring Pakistan.

TURKIYE MAARIF FOUNDATION ISLAMABAD OFFICE

Founded through an ordinance enacted on June 28, 2016, as a 'subsidiary' of the Turkish Ministry of National Education, the Turkiye Maarif Foundation (TMF) outgrew its parent organization by the measure of being labeled as 'the parallel Turkish Ministry of National Education'. Started with the seed money earmarked from the Ministry and later sponsored through miscellaneous official and unofficial sources, the TMF dispatched its representatives to Pakistan and started working at the Turkish Embassy in Islamabad almost immediately after its inception before the July 2016 coup attempt. Formalized within the framework of an accelerated protocol and special instructions issued by the Federal Ministry of Education and the Ministry of Interior in Islamabad prior to Erdogan's

November 2016 visit, the TMF started negotiations with the Pakistani authorities to take over the PakTurk Schools. They also talked to the Turkish journalists intermittently about their progress in this process.

On November 17, 2016, Hürriyet columnist Vahap Munyar, who accompanied Erdogan's official delegation to Pakistan, penned an article from Islamabad mentioning that the TMF Pakistan Representative explained to him how the PakTurk Schools would be taken over.

Unable to take over the schools immediately, the TMF kept looking for intermediate solutions and met with the representatives of various religious communities active in the education sector, trying to establish a network. They were so confident about taking over the schools shortly that they even started meeting with political Islamist groups, in particular to find local administrators and teachers loyal to them when they could take the schools over. This even heartened some Islamist groups to circulate WhatsApp messages saying, *"We need teachers for our forthcoming schools. Those interested must write to such-and-such e-mail address,"* which revealed their institutions had been in liaison with the TMF.

Having publicized their arrival in the media, the TMF officials kept trying to convince the PakTurk parents with prospective offers like 50% discount on fees and generous scholarships for the PakTurk students who wished to study at the Turkish universities, once the schools would be handed over.

A Pakistani journalist interviewed the Turkish Ambassador in Islamabad Sadık Babür Girgin for an online TV channel and asked him, "What changes will take place in PakTurk if the Maarif Foundation takes over the schools?" He replied, "The students in the schools will be given scholarships and they will also be offered to have their university education in Turkiye on scholarship." The concerned people in Pakistan were aware of the circumstances. Contrary to what the TMF presented as an incentive, the PakTurk educational institutions had been offering their students merits scholarship for the last 20-odd years. It was obvious that the TMF "would not be content with usurping the PakTurk Schools; they would also steal their education model and showcase it as if it was their own."

Since the day it arrived in Pakistan, the TMF exerted pressure on the Pakistani federal and provincial governments to place the PakTurk Schools and their management in difficulty. Oddly enough, the otherwise-aloof Turkish Ambassador and the Turkish Embassy personnel – be they diplomats or the contracted staff – spent much time out of office in field work for stoking the Erdogan regime's discourse against the PakTurk Schools in the Pakistani public and official opinion. In the future, when researchers study this transactional segment of the Pakistan-Turkiye relations, they will unveil the shameful and rude campaign conducted in Pakistan by the Turkish operatives.

TOP-DOWN TRUSTEES FOR THE PAKTURK SCHOOLS

On August 25, 2016, one month before the expiry of the Turkish educators' visas and residence permits, a group of

PakTurk management was invited to Lahore by Rana Sanaullah Khan, the then-Law Minister of the Punjab Province.

Rana Sanaullah Khan requested something unexpected from the PakTurk executives. The Minister proposed to the delegation that the four Turkish citizens on PakTurk Schools' Board of Directors be removed and replaced with four Pakistani citizens of the Government of Punjab's choice. He also 'recommended' that all members of the seven-member Board of Directors of the PakTurk Foundation be Pakistani citizens. The PakTurk officials at the meeting said such a change would create further problems and will also leave several problems unresolved. They told Rana Sanaullah Khan the visas and the residence permits of the Turkish educators had yet to be renewed despite their imminent expiry within a month, and explained it would be difficult to accept the request under these circumstances.

In response, Rana Sanaullah Khan vouched for the renewal of the visas and residency permits of the Turkish educators and claimed that since the Punjab Chief Minister Shehbaz Sharif was to visit Turkiye to attend the inauguration ceremony of the Yavuz Sultan Selim Bridge, this 'request' had no ulterior motives, but only their sincere wish to strengthen the Punjab Chief Minister's hand before his visit to Turkiye and help reduce the pressure from Turkish authorities. After holding discussions and believing in the Minister's personal promise about the visa extensions, the members of the PakTurk Board of Directors consented to the proposed change as 'requested'.

Following the resignation of the Turkish members of the Board of Directors, the three members appointed by the

Government of the Punjab arrived at the PakTurk Education Foundation Head Office in Islamabad. One was appointed as the CEO of the Foundation. On the day of the meeting, I welcomed the new members of the Foundation myself. After greeting him, the new CEO told me he would rush to a meeting with the Turkish Ambassador at the Turkish Embassy immediately after the meeting at the Foundation. The personal promise made by the Punjab Law Minister that no harm would come to the PakTurk Schools if their request was fulfilled culminated with the appointment of a new CEO in connivance with the Turkish Embassy Islamabad. Blurting out his next meeting just as he arrived, the new CEO owned up in a way that he was hand in glove with the Turkish Embassy in Islamabad and inadvertently delivered the update of what ominous consequences were in store for the PakTurk Schools.

In the second meeting, the two newly-appointed members and the CEO proposed the appointment of a new member to the Board of Directors, a Turkish citizen recommended by the Turkish Embassy Islamabad, despite the 'request' of the Punjab Law Minister for an 'all-Pakistani' Board of Directors. Unable to have the PakTurk Schools through official channels, the TMF planned to materialize its objective by infiltrating the institutions from a top position of the Board. Sensing the unfolding intrigue, Alamgir Khan, Chairman of the PakTurk Education Foundation, said these proposals could not be entertained in ongoing meetings with preset agenda as per the rules and postponed the discussion to a later date, frustrating the Embassy's attempt.

Eventually, the nefarious plans of the members appointed

by deception did not work out, and Chairman Alamgir Khan appealed to the Administrative Court on behalf of the PakTurk Schools stating that the PakTurk Education Foundation's property and administrative rights had been violated. The posts of the Government of the Punjab-appointed board members were revoked by the Court.

PUNJAB PROVINCIAL OFFICIALS

Mian Muhammad Shehbaz Sharif, the current Prime Minister and the former Chief Minister Punjab, has not only been a political ally to Erdogan, but also a close business partner. At times, Erdogan made Lahore-exclusive visits to Pakistan, only to meet Shehbaz Sharif.

Not content with the plain friendship of the two countries, Shehbaz Sharif was keen on investing in Turkiye. Sharif and Erdogan developed deeper relationships in person and business. Knowing his younger brother Shehbaz's closeness with Erdogan, Prime Minister Nawaz Sharif wanted him to address the PakTurk issue. When his attempts to use the full extent of his powers to force the PakTurk Schools to be handed over to the Maarif Foundation did not work, Shehbaz Sharif called in law enforcement agencies loyal to his party. Officials from the Punjab Counter-Terrorism Department targeted the members of the PakTurk Education Foundation's Board of Directors and in particular the Chairman, Alamgir Khan.

The request for a change in the members of the Board of Directors had been made by a Punjab provincial government official. When the ultimate goal of appointing the Maarif

Foundation's country representative in Islamabad to the Board of Directors failed, they summoned Mr. Alamgir Khan, a 70-plus gentleman from the notables of Islamabad, to Lahore, a journey of 4 hours and 400 kilometers from Islamabad, to join a meeting at the Chief Minister's Secretariat. After making him wait in an office until evening, they sent him back saying "The person who would meet you has not been available". When this perpetuated almost every week between December 2016 and February 2017, Mr. Alamgir Khan complained to the authorities. When he was summoned to Lahore with the promise that the meeting would definitely take place, Mr. Alamgir Khan reached the secretariat. The officials, who had thought Chairman Khan would surely give up one day due to his age, noticed the failure of their scheme and so changed strategy.

Besides such forceful and grueling intercity travels which he mostly made solo, Mr. Alamgir Khan was also distressed with psychological harassment and threats for a long period. After frequent summons to the Chief Minister's Office in Lahore, he was also summoned by the Punjab Counter-Terrorism Department to give a statement on the grounds of "an investigation initiated against him pursuant to a criminal complaint". After long interrogations and investigations, the Counter-Terrorism Department, unable to find "anything adequately incriminating" Mr. Alamgir Khan, forwarded the matter to the Financial Crimes Investigation Department hoping that "they may find some financial discrepancies". The authorities there attempted to intimidate Mr. Alamgir Khan by demanding miscellaneous documents frequently. One day they demanded to scrutinize the accounting books of the schools, another day they wanted to run through the payrolls of the Turkish staff, another day they wanted to double-check the title deeds and the installment payments of the school plots, and kept demanding other details and files. Having witnessed of Mr. Alamgir Khan's forbearance against these harassments and intimidation attempts and his strong resolve in defending the PakTurk Schools under his management, the officials decided to reveal their "trump card" as mentioned above.

As promised, the officials met Mr. Alamgir Khan at the meeting venue on time and told him they would like to discuss the matter over dinner. When Mr. Alamgir Khan asked to discuss the agenda, the officials were nonchalant and simply said, "Why do you ever care about this matter?" Without bothering to listen to what Mr. Alamgir Khan had to say, one official interjected that they wanted Mr. Alamgir to resign from the management of the PakTurk Schools. When Mr. Alamgir said he would not consider resigning, the officials attempted to intimidate him with a pistol they put on the table. "If you do not resign, we are not responsible for the things to happen," they threatened. "I am a mortal past his seventy years, someone who has achieved everything he wished in life, someone who is at the death's door! Whatever you say, I am not scared!", Mr. Alamgir retorted and left the table without looking back, enraging his interlocutors.

Seeing that the Punjab administration kept complicating things instead of being the part of solution, Mr. Alamgir Khan moved the Administrative Court the day after the incident. The judge ruled in Mr. Alamgir Khan's favor, citing the circumstances forced upon the PakTurk Schools and the

PakTurk Education Foundation and the coerced nature of the appointment of board members by the Punjab administration, and revoked the appointments. The same court ordered an official writ to be dispatched to all official departments in the Punjab, including law enforcement entities. The court also ruled that Mr. Alamgir Khan should not be harassed and that no demands should be made of him without the court's acknowledgment. After the announcement of the verdict, the judge said to the usher, "Call the reporters into the courtroom," and told the journalists to report on the case, explaining to them the unlawful treatments against Mr. Alamgir Khan.

As if the threats of the Punjab provincial government were not enough, the officials also blocked the bank accounts of Mr. Alamgir Khan, a prominent businessman. Despite the surveillance imposed on his house, Mr. Alamgir Khan remained steadfast and defended the PakTurk Schools as a true hero throughout.

SOUTH ASIA CENTER FOR STRATEGIC RESEARCH (GASAM)

The mindset behind the AKP had established institutions that could be used by the Turkish political Islamist thought, especially in recent times, for the dissemination and unconditional acceptance of Erdogan's expansionist political approach in Pakistan. GASAM holds a prominent place among these "think-tanks". Founded by AKP Gaziantep MP Ali Şahin, who received education in Pakistan during the early 1990s provided key inspiration for the AKP's transactional approach to Pakistan.

In their publications and research dossiers, GASAM has evaluated Pakistan in terms of "why and how Turkiye can increase its reception across the country with its ideological political approach". GASAM's hand in glove relations with the incumbent regime in Turkiye were also revealed through Erdogan's son-in-law Berat Albayrak's leaked emails by Wikileaks in recent years, especially the consultative status undertaken by the GASAM on how the Erdogan regime can set agenda in Pakistan. Berat Albayrak's emails and the ensuing steps taken by the AKP regime in Pakistan suggested how the Turkish Islamist politics shaped by the AKP could be introduced in Pakistan and how the Pakistani media was managed through specially created news reports, given the AKP's political perception.

That Berat Albayrak, the erstwhile minister, was informed in detail about the news items and columns published in Pakistani – and even in Indian – press against the Hizmet Movement and was asked for his opinion on the effective and powerful spread of the political ideology of his father-in-law, President Erdogan, in and around Pakistan must be because of the key importance the incumbent regime attaches to the Islamist elements in Pakistan for consolidating their myths. Having received an augmented attention from Turkiye when it needed the most, Pakistan could remain relevant in regional and world politics with the outward support provided by Turkiye, especially in the Kashmir cause. Pakistan kept on its foreign policy with relative gains in return for great concessions it made by pursuing a "balanced policy" between Turkiye, Iran, and Saudi Arabia which have always wished to have a say in the region.

In 2016, when the media worldwide ran headlines like "Is Erdogan becoming Turkiye's Zia-ul-Haq?" and "Turkiye is becoming Pakistanized", the GASAM published an article titled, "Turkiye is Setting an Example for Pakistan". This piece also demonstrated GASAM's romanticized view to Pakistan, a major country in one of the world's most volatile geographies, and how distant from the truth by hinting no other regional actor than Turkiye impacted Pakistan more. In this context, Erdogan's view of Pakistan as a crucial nation to be won for his ideological expansionist policy in the region heralded yet another major crisis for the Hizmet Movement, which has been dedicated to bringing forth free-thinking individuals who are an antidote to the radicalism and violence plaguing the region.

ERDOGAN: CONQUEROR OF KASHMIR (!)

After the partition between Pakistan and India in 1947, Kashmir has been at the forefront of unresolved border and territorial disputes. Since 1948, Pakistan's persistent attempts at the United Nations for Kashmir to choose the country it would join through a popular referendum have been fruitless and the predominantly Muslim region has remained a bleeding wound. The Kashmir issue bears serious similarities with Turkiye's Cyprus issue.

Towards the end of the 1930s, Britain increasingly lost its almost century-long uncontested dominance of the Indian subcontinent. As the days of British "withdrawal from the Pearl of the Crown" approached, the differences of opinion between Gandhi and Muhammad Ali Jinnah became more intense. Particularly from 1940 onwards, Jinnah became more vocal for the creation of a Muslim state. Pakistan was founded in 1947 as an independent state in a geographical area covering the territory of present-day Pakistan and Bangladesh. Kashmir remains a disputed territory to this day. Under the treaties, 565 large and small principalities in the Indian subcontinent, inhabited by 99 million people, chose between India and Pakistan primarily based on religious, ethnic, and geographical factors. The Hindu prince of Jammu and Kashmir, a Muslim-majority state caught between the two countries, could not decide which country to join until the last day. After signing an agreement with Pakistan to avoid interruptions in trade, travel, and communication, the prince prolonged the issue of accession. In the wake of the reported intensive attacks on Muslims in the region, thousands of armed men from Pashtun tribes living in West Pakistan entered Kashmir in October 1947. The prince of Jammu and Kashmir then summoned the Indian government for help, leading to the first war between Pakistan and India. In 1948, the UN proposed a referendum, but the mistrust between the two countries and India's harsh stance led to years of massacres and disenfranchisement of Muslims living in Kashmir. Kashmiri Muslims are still subjected to constant harassment and assimilation.

On May 4, 2017, Erdogan made an ambitious claim that he could be a mediator between India and Pakistan for resolving the Kashmir conflict. He subsequently visited India. Knowing full well that he would return empty-handed, Erdogan was keen to exploit this trip to send a message to boost his popularity in Pakistan. It is also telling these developments coincided with Erdogan's efforts for having the PakTurk Schools transferred to the TMF.

Erdogan met with Prime Minister Modi during his visit to India. He expressed his willingness to help solve the Kashmir issue. The Indian Prime Minister expressed his skepticism and added: "Before you visit, I wished to know about the number of think tanks in Turkiye on Kashmir and the scope of research conducted on this issue. I learned that Turkiye has no institution on Kashmir and that a few academic research was conducted. How can you arbitrate on an issue your country is so unfamiliar with?" Modi rejected Erdogan's initiative, sending a clear message that the pompous politics prevalent in Turkiye would not find an audience in India, or if it would ever, it would be made in India.

Notwithstanding, Erdogan achieved his goal. Even though he failed to achieve results in India, he managed to get himself on the agenda in both Turkiye and Pakistan with the Kashmir issue. Modi's advice must have paid off, as think tanks on Kashmir, which had not been opened in Turkiye until then, mushroomed one after another in universities and elsewhere under the auspices of the Erdogan's party AKP.

Chapter 3

Faux Coup in Turkiye and
Repercussions in Pakistan

(July 15, 2016 –
November 15, 2016)

After an all-star 18-year success until 2013, PakTurk Schools were targeted by exclusive fear and intimidation between 2013 and 2016 because of the repressive Erdogan regime in Turkiye. During this period, the AKP strategically and steadily harassed the PakTurk Schools. The steps taken against the PakTurk School between 2013 and 2016 can be listed as follows:

❖ Removal of the PakTurk staff from the invitation lists of the Turkish Embassy in Islamabad and the Turkish Consulate in Karachi,

❖ Discrimination against the PakTurk graduates. PakTurk graduates who often acted as interpreters during the visits of Turkish officials to Pakistan were no longer invited to the programs, and the PakTurk graduates who applied for the Turkiye Scholarships were eliminated despite their high scores.

❖ Field visits by the Embassy staff to discredit the PakTurk Schools,

❖ Suspension of the PakTurk Education Foundation's in-progress school and university projects,

❖ Non-renewal of visas and residence permits of the Turkish educators,

❖ By distorting the final declaration of the Foreign Ministers Meeting of the Organization of Islamic Cooperation in October 2016, slandering the Turkish educators working in the PakTurk Schools with terrorism charges in the Pakistani public opinion to expedite the unlawful transfer of the PakTurk schools to the Maarif Foundation and pave the way for the deportation of Turkish educators from Pakistan,

❖ Lobbying for the closure of the PakTurk Schools.

These strategies were fast-tracked between November 2016 and December 2017 with constant changes in the oppression format:

❖ Revocation of the visas and residence permits and the forced deportation of the Turkish educators working in the PakTurk Schools,

❖ Deliberately denying consular services to Turkish educators working in the PakTurk Schools, contrary to their basic citizenship rights,

❖ Announcing that the schools would be "gifted" to the Government of Pakistan or some local communities after their transfer to the Maarif Foundation to gain the support of the Pakistani public opinion,

❖ Special efforts and funding by the Turkish Embassy in Islamabad to take government officials, opinion leaders, and members of the media from Pakistan to Turkiye and expose them to the regime-managed post-July 2016 perception there to gain support in the Pakistani media for transferring the PakTurk Schools to the Maarif Foundation,

❖ Encouraging the Government of Pakistan to change the provisions of the commercial law preventing the state from forcibly seizing foundations and companies, leading to a midnight amendment attempt to Pakistan's Companies Act,

❖ Intensifying efforts to have the PakTurk Schools transferred to the Maarif Foundation instead of closing them down,

❖ Causing fear and anxiety among parents by using

connections in the Pakistani media and spreading regime-concocted news stories against the PakTurk educational institutions in the Pakistani print, visual, and Internet media and the social media accounts of pro-Erdogan Pakistani academics and other professionals living in Turkiye and elsewhere,

❖ Sabotaging the Board of Directors of the PakTurk Education Foundation through the intervention of the Government of the Punjab officials to have the schools transferred to the Maarif Foundation by infiltrating the Board,

❖ The Maarif Foundation's attempt to become a party of the court case filed by the PakTurk Schools, claiming to be the real owner of the schools,

❖ Harassing the PakTurk Education Foundation board members through the Punjab provincial law enforcement agencies when their plans were disrupted or delayed,

❖ Bringing government officials of all levels from Turkiye under the guise of official visits and deploying them to apply pressure on the Pakistani authorities,

❖ Deploying all means at the disposal of the Turkish Ministry of Foreign Affairs to cancel the UNHCR's decision to grant asylum seeker certificates to the Turkish educators working at the PakTurk Schools, attempting to pressurize the UNHCR into reversing this decision, or prevent the renewal of their asylum certificates in any case,

❖ Inviting the Turkish National Intelligence Agency (MIT) operatives under the guise of an official mission and attempting to abduct the PakTurk Education Foundation executives,

❖ Taking the Government of the Punjab elite law enforcement entities on board when the Turkish intelligence operatives' direct abduction attempt failed.

After the revocation of their visas and residence in November 2016 and the abduction of a Turkish educator couple with their two daughters from Lahore to Turkiye by a joint operation of the Turkish and Pakistani intelligence elements in September 2017, the remaining Turkish educators left Pakistan to the third countries before the expiry of their passports and asylum seeker certificates in 2018 and 2019. Only one hindrance stood on the path of the Turkish Embassy Islamabad to achieve its goal: Having the PakTurk Schools transferred to the Maarif Foundation. The strategies (!) followed by the Embassy included:

❖ Having Pakistan's payment of 1.2 billion dollars in compensation to the Karkey Karadeniz Elektrik waived in exchange for transferring the PakTurk Schools to the Maarif Foundation,

❖ Visits to the Army Headquarters and the Supreme Court of Pakistan, the most powerful institutions of the country, to hold persuasive meetings with the Commander of the Army Staff, the Chief of General Staff, and the Chief Justice of the Supreme Court.

❖ Attempts to have the Supreme Court of Pakistan declare the Hizmet Movement as a so-called 'terrorist' organization in Pakistan by submitting a falsified version of the October 2016 final declaration of the Organization of Islamic Unity.

Turkish Embassy in Islamabad considered it a foremost duty to have the PakTurk Schools transferred to the TMF and the Turkish educators expelled from Pakistan through constant pressures and intrigues. Working overtime, the Embassy personnel not only made several civilians and officials in Pakistan complicit in its own crimes through intrigues and kickbacks, but also committed irreparable felonies. Disregarding the local and international laws and bilateral agreements, it violated basic freedoms and rights to ownerships, besides damaging Turkiye's hard-earned egalitarian standing for a repressive regime.

The Turkish Embassy and Consulate officials, whose taxpayer-sponsored overseas diplomatic mission primarily consists of catering to the official matters of the Turkish citizens abroad and facilitating them as per their innate citizenship rights, worked day and night by a 'devotion' bordering the 'joy of worship' to neutralize the Hizmet participants, who effectively represented their home country as cultural ambassadors and won the admiration of locals with their commendable conduct. In a holier-than-thou attitude, the Turkish foreign mission officials dedicated themselves to enacting the repressive measures of the Erdogan regime for disrupting the activities of numerous highly-appreciated educational institutions founded and operated through hard work worldwide by thousands of people. This way, they perhaps broke new ground in sacrificing diplomatic ethics to sheer partisanship and have themselves recorded in the modern annals of history. It is certain when the historians in future will delve deeper to explore the details of the repressive acts perpetrated by the Turkish foreign missions in Pakistan and elsewhere, they will discover myriad stories and consequences for the world to know.

This section will focus on the events from November 2016, when the Government of Pakistan decreed to deport the Turkish educators working at the PakTurk Schools, to September 2017. This period will also be remembered for the tragic human tragedies and callous international crimes committed by the two countries.

In early November 2016, Erdogan's official visit to Islamabad was finalized. Following the Turkish Foreign Minister Mevlüt Çavuşoğlu's visit to Pakistan in August 2016, the fate of the PakTurk Schools and the post-July 2016 tensions found extensive coverage in the Pakistani media. Journalists visiting the PakTurk Education Foundation interviewed the Foundation executives and the school administrators across Pakistan. Meanwhile, the Foundation took concerted precautions to protect the institutions against an illegal transfer and ensure the Turkish educators could continue their duties.

We learned from Mr. Alamgir Khan, then Chairman of the PakTurk Schools, that he received a call from an American official from the United Nations Islamabad Office a few days before Mr. Erdogan's visit in November 2016. When the official asked Mr. Khan if he could visit the United Nations Office in the Diplomatic Enclave for an interview, Mr. Alamgir said he would be happy to meet with him, but that if he came to the PakTurk Education Foundation head office, he could see the schools and that they could also conduct the requested interview. Accordingly, the official arrived at the PakTurk Head Office around 2:00 p.m. on the same day in an official car with United Nations license plates and we welcomed him at the door. When we met, he told us he was a diplomat of the US Embassy Islamabad and that he came to have information about the recent news about the PakTurk Schools. After a brief introduction to the school, I took him to Mr. Alamgir Khan's office. We witnessed that the American diplomat, who we thought was there to receive information, had come to the meeting well-prepared. First, he asked Mr. Alamgir for information about the latest situation of the PakTurk Schools. He asked about the stance of the Government of Pakistan. To this question, Mr. Alamgir said, "We are in constant touch with the respective government departments and authorities. They tell us that the issue is political and that the schools will be inflicted no harm," to which the visitor replied, "We also consider it political." The American diplomat said that before coming to the meeting, he had posed the same question to a Pakistani diplomat at the Ministry of Foreign Affairs and the Pakistani diplomat said they had no agenda to close the schools. The American diplomat said, "I checked your website before coming here and you posted that your institutions are not affiliated with Mr. Gulen. I would like to ask you about this." Mr. Alamgir said, "Yes, our institutions do not have direct and organic ties with Mr. Gulen in terms of physical, financial, and human resources, but Mr. Gulen is a person like our country's national poet, Allama Dr. Muhammad Iqbal, whom everyone in Turkiye knows, reads his books and draws inspiration from." In response, the American diplomat asked, "Are Mr. Gulen's books taught in your schools? Are his philosophy and ideas taught to the students in the curriculum?" Mr. Alamgir told the diplomat that the PakTurk Schools follow the official Pakistani curriculum and the Cambridge O and A Level curriculum, that they teach nothing about Turkiye, and therefore there is no question of Mr. Gulen's books or his teachings being taught. After this brief meeting, the diplomat asked for permission to leave, expressing his good wishes.

The journalists who visited the PakTurk Schools always asked to know whether our institutions had direct contact with Mr. Gulen. The fallacy that blamed Mr. Fethullah Gulen and the Hizmet Movement for the July 15 faux coup with no evidence was served to the Pakistani media by the Turkish Embassy Islamabad. During his July 22, 2016 press conference, the Turkish Ambassador in Islamabad lied that the revenue from the PakTurk educational institutions was transferred abroad, especially to Mr. Gulen. When a journalist from The News International, a national English-language newspaper, wanted to have answers to his questions, the Foundation executives referred him to me. While I thought I would be bombarded with various questions, the journalist kept asking me the same question for 30 minutes: "Are the PakTurk Schools connected to Gulen?" He even went the extra mile in asking, "Look, I am asking you this as a friend, you can tell me this, you do not need to hide it." Although I told him that Mr. Gulen was an authoritative Muslim scholar with talks broadcast on televisions and books widely available almost in every household in Turkiye, and that people listen to his talks and read from his books occasionally, he said, "No, this is not the answer I want. I want an answer about Mr. Gulen's relationship and link with your institutions."

108 of the 1500 personnel of the PakTurk educational institutions were from Turkiye. An overwhelming majority of the teaching and administrative staff – including the senior administrators like principals, vice principals, heads

of departments, and education coordinators – serving approximately 11000 students in 28 schools were Pakistani. Having started by the end of 2013 and kept escalating with the opening of the schools in August 2016 in the wake of the dastardly June 15, 2016 incident, the pressure from the Turkish Embassy Islamabad made itself felt in several aspects.

One of the Turkish Embassy's biggest lies was the claim that the PakTurk Schools were run under the auspices of the Çağ Education Foundation in Istanbul. In the wake of the July 15, 2016 coup conspiracy, thousands of educational institutions in Turkiye were seized and closed for their alleged links to the Hizmet Movement. The Turkish Ambassador spread the lie that the seized Çağ Education Foundation had been transferred to the Government of Turkiye and therefore the PakTurk Schools in Pakistan should be transferred to the Maarif Foundation founded in Turkiye. The PakTurk Schools had long been owned by a local foundation established by Pakistani businessmen since 2013, long before the coup attempt. The official transfer process was authorized by the Securities & Exchange Commission (SECP) of Pakistan and the PakTurk Schools were owned by a foundation founded and operated by Pakistani citizens. Notwithstanding the official documents and official confirmation by the respective commission, the Turkish Embassy in Islamabad maintained this narrative and kept this baseless claim on the agenda for having the PakTurk Schools transferred.

On August 2, 2016, erstwhile Foreign Minister Çavuşoğlu visited Pakistan to discuss the transfer of the PakTurk Schools and met with his Pakistani counterpart Sartaj Aziz. When Çavuşoğlu demanded the extradition of the Turkish teachers from Pakistan, Sartaj Aziz, erstwhile Advisor to the Prime Minister on Foreign Affairs who also served as the Minister of Finance, Minister of Foreign Affairs, and National Security Advisor in earlier governments, had been briefed by his advisors that such unwarranted extradition would violate international laws. Sartaj Aziz reiterated this to the Turkish FM and said it would be impossible to fulfill this request as demanded. The press conference after the bilateral meeting garnered intense media interest as both ministers were also asked about the fate of the PakTurk Schools. While Çavuşoğlu imputed the PakTurk Schools and Turkish educators, Sartaj Aziz said, "There is no question of closing the schools; we are working on alternative solutions that will not disrupt the education of students."

The day after the press conference, PakTurk Education Foundation's head office received an intense flow of journalists. Following the press statement from the Ministry of Foreign Affairs, the members of the PakTurk Schools Parent-Teacher Association issued a statement on August 9, 2016, expressing their distress and utter concern over the incidents and emphasized that the PakTurk Schools and the students must never be drawn in political disputes. The parents demanded the Government of Pakistan to take prudent measures so as not to be implicated in Turkiye's political issues and act against the interest of the citizens of Pakistan. They also called for an end to the unpleasant interventions and political statements.

After the parent-teacher conference, local and international media organizations expressed their interest in interviewing the students, teachers, and parents at the schools, and our institutions opened their doors to all media members for a day. Local media outlets such as Dawn, The News International, The Nation, Roznama Jang, Dawn TV, Geo TV, Dunya TV, Urdu One and international media outlets such as AFP, AP, Reuters, BBC Urdu, Voice of America, Washington Post and The New York Times interviewed students, teachers, and parents and shared the events with the global public opinion.

When the BBC Urdu contacted my school and asked for an interview, I gave them an appointment and a reporter arrived. The BBC Urdu reporter said the BBC World asked them to prepare a special report on the PakTurk Schools across Pakistan and they would file a collective news report on the international Turkish schools targeted by the Erdogan regime worldwide. We explained what we knew about the crisis and the BBC Urdu prepared an in-depth news report. They said they would also like to visit a student's home and interview them. A segment including the student's morning preparation for the school, having breakfast, and getting on the school bus was embedded in short interviews with students and parents about the recent events. BBC World published this comprehensive report about the PakTurk Schools on its website and regional bulletins.

As the PakTurk Schools issue remained a hot topic in the Pakistani media, the Turkish Embassy in Islamabad's deceptive propaganda continued unabated, claiming that not only most principals were Turkish, but also the actual owner of the schools was the Istanbul-based Çağ Education Foundation, of which assets were seized by the regime after the July 15 coup attempt, and therefore the PakTurk Schools should be transferred to the state-sponsored Maarif Foundation.

Following Çavuşoğlu's visit and as a response to the lies spread by the Turkish Embassy Islamabad, the PakTurk Education Foundation Board of Directors appointed Pakistani principals to all PakTurk Schools.

Gradually implemented for long as a policy of the Foundation to train and appoint the local colleagues to the positions of principal and deputy principal, the change of school principals was carried out smoothly and with the consent of the parent representatives. This way, the new arrangement caused no panic among the students or parents. When some ill-thinking people informed the Turkish Embassy about this step, the Embassy had the English daily Dawn, report that "Turkish Principals Removed from PakTurk Schools" on August 10, 2016. The Embassy passed the ball to Turkiye and all news channels reported that Turkish educators had been removed from PakTurk Schools for possible ties with Fethullah Gulen. The news spread around the world in a short time and assumed different titles depending on the media outlets' objectivity or proximity with the Erdogan regime. Friends worldwide phoned to know about the latest developments. I cannot forget an incident, which still pains me in the heart. Having watched the news about our schools, my sister phoned me from Turkiye and wept, "This world's so full of evil! What do they want from you?" The timing was rather significant in showing how an ordinary administrative step taken by the PakTurk Schools had been distorted by the Turkish Embassy Islamabad and conveyed inversely to Turkiye.

Despite all odds, the PakTurk Schools did not back down and, on August 10, 2016, appointed Pakistani educators as principals in all PakTurk educational institutions, thus frustrating the intrigues on the institutions. The Foundation's gradual policy of localization through training the Pakistani staff for the administrative positions and streamlining all PakTurk Schools under the management of Pakistani principals was thus implemented immediately. No matter how sudden it was, the change was well received by the students and parents.

About three weeks after Çavuşoğlu's visit, it was announced that the then-Punjab Chief Minister Shehbaz Sharif would attend the August 26, 2016 inauguration of the Yavuz Sultan Selim Bridge, which Erdogan touted as one of his "giant projects". Soon, a rumor circulated that Rana Sanaullah Khan, then-Punjab Law Minister and a close aide to Shehbaz Sharif, wished to have an urgent meeting with the PakTurk Education Foundation executives before the Chief Minister's trip. There was not a single day without a new development or crisis.

It was no secret that the Government of Pakistan kept stalling the Turkish educators on this issue. Punjab Law Minister Rana Sanaullah demanded the resignation of the Turkish directors in the PakTurk Education Foundation Board of Directors in exchange for the renewal of the Turkish educators' visas and residence permits. He also said they wished to appoint three Pakistani citizens as board members – read "trustees" – in place of the outgoing Turkish directors. Despite their concerns, the Turkish board directors in the PakTurk Education Foundation agreed to the Minister's demands to protect the ownership of the institutions and to have the visa renewal issue resolved.

Turkish board directors of the PakTurk Education Foundation resigned before Shehbaz Sharif's departure for Turkiye. After the first meeting with the new members appointed by the Punjab government, the PakTurk Board of Directors sensed that the government would not keep its promise on visa renewals. Things were getting more complicated.

September 9, 2016, the date of visa and residence permit expiry, arrived. The Pakistani authorities deliberately had not taken a positive step and left the matter in limbo. Keeping Turkish educators employed in the institutions without visas from that day on was discussed with the corporate legal advisors. While the Foundation management wanted to file an official application, the legal advisors stated that since there was no final decision by the Government of Pakistan, "Turkish teachers could continue to work officially".

Although the prevailing legal guidance was that the Turkish teachers could continue to work in the institutions without visas, this uncertainty also had a grave impact on the Turkish educators. They wanted the issue to be resolved without delay. PakTurk Education Foundation management deliberated on multiple alternatives to extend the visas. One alternative was to move the courts for the matter.

Sensing the solemnity of the PakTurk Schools management, the Ministry of Interior officials intervened and conveyed verbally that "there was no need to move the courts and that the Turkish teachers could continue to work as they were until the resolution of the matter." What's more, they said they kept "holding up the visa renewal process to dissipate the pressure from Turkiye."

The judicial independence in Pakistan back then was significantly solid. In those days, the government was facing corruption allegations. The officials did not wish to deal with the consequences of the visa renewal crisis of the Turkish educators as an additional headache.

At the verbal request from the Ministry of Interior officials who gave the signals that the issue could soon be resolved and reiterated an official position that the visa renewal procedures were delayed due to pressure from Turkiye, the PakTurk management temporarily shelved its decision to take the visa renewal crisis to court. It was decided to follow the government's recommendations.

Despite the expiry of the visas on September 9, 2016, the government dragged the matter out. This continued for two months until November 15, 2016. Meanwhile, they tried their best to drop the visa renewal crisis of the Turkish educators and the fate of the PakTurk Schools from the national agenda.

The delaying tactics of the Government of Pakistan officials towards the Turkish Embassy's intense requests on behalf of the Government of Turkiye between September 9 and November 15, 2016 surged reactions from the Erdogan regime. The Turkish Ambassador in Islamabad, overwhelmed by the adjourning attitude of the Ministry of Foreign Affairs, soon started to behave in ways trespassing the diplomatic norms. In the words of a Pakistani MoFA official, Turkish Ambassador Sadık Babür Girgin, furious and patronizing, attempted to hold the Pakistani officials to account several times as if he was a "viceroy".

Meanwhile, PakTurk educational institutions intensified their educational activities to reduce tensions and increase the students' motivation.

DEPORTATION PHASE

During this period, the Federal Minister of Education and a young MP from the opposition party PTI were among the parents of our school. As the Federal Minister of Education, Muhammad Baligh-ur-Rehman was the government's façade to answer the most questions about the PakTurk Schools. Amidst the crisis, he wanted his children's education to continue in our schools. On January 7, 2016, despite intense pressure from the Turkish Embassy, the Federal Minister of Education attended PakTurk Schools' National Inter-School Mathematics Olympiad (ISMO) Award Ceremony as the chief guest, handed out awards to the high-achieving students and spoke highly of the PakTurk Schools. Another parent, Shehryar Afridi, an opposition member of the National Assembly of Pakistan, visited our school after returning from an event in the UK House of Lords and claimed all problems faced by the PakTurk Schools originated from the Nawaz Sharif government and the Sharif family's close relations with the Erdogan family. He claimed he had also mentioned the PakTurk Schools issue in his speech at the House of Lords where he had referred to his children and said "My two angels are deeply saddened by the unfair governance of the country and the crisis faced by their school."

Around that time, Erdogan was preparing for an exclusive official visit to Pakistan. It was rumored he would discuss with his Pakistani interlocutors why the government of Pakistan had not yet responded positively to his demands for the handover of the PakTurk Schools, and that he would assert this demand at the highest level. Confirming this notion was a column written by İlnur Çevik, then-Chief Advisor to Erdogan, in Yeni Birlik newspaper after attending a business conference on the invitation of the UMT (University of Management and Technology) in Lahore on November 7-8, 2016, just a week before Erdogan's official visit. In his column, Çevik wrote, "PakTurk Schools still continue their education, and the Pakistani government still does not respond favorably to the Turkish government's requests. This means Mr. President will pull the ears of some during his visit to Pakistan within a week's time."

Erdogan's visit in November 2016 re-bled a fretting crisis that had even scabbed over to some extent. Everyone wondered about the potential changes in the attitude of the Pakistani authorities prompted by the visit, and they kept appraising likely scenarios. The Turkish educators were immensely concerned. Some local colleagues even voiced that the Pakistani government might hand over the schools and deport all Turkish educators. A mere talk of this peaked tensions.

The frequency of meetings at the PakTurk Education Foundation head office increased as they sought to know what the Government of Pakistan thought about the issue. As a parent holding a prominent post in the government, then-Federal Minister of Education Muhammad Baligh-ur-Rehman displayed his political side and did not show his true colors as he sent the message, "Everything is going fine."

Giving no secrets on this issue, he seemed to say "There is no need to worry."

Despite the speculations fueled by Erdogan's arrival, no Turkish educator left Pakistan since none had committed anything against the law either in Turkiye or Pakistan. They felt at ease and, relying on the rule of law, they kept waiting. Actually, Pakistan would soon witness scene after scene the heroism of 108 Turkish educators and their families that will go down in history with great praise. Commendable were the stance and patience of the devoted educators. On one side was the Erdogan regime, which trampled on the international law and Turkiye's progressive reputation by mobilizing all state apparatus for repression at home and abroad. On the other side were the Turkish educators representing Turkiye in Pakistan for years and leading their students from one success to another. This noble legion of educators, on whom both governments disproportionately exerted full-court pressure with myriad elements to force them to flee, conquered hearts and minds with their active patience throughout the crisis. They were the practitioners and living witnesses of how true men and women of heart can be when the world's troubles and hardships kept piling upon them, increasing the pressures beyond human endurance. In full view of Pakistan and the world, they demonstrated the attributes of the golden generation to the friend and the foe with their silent cries when the pressures and oppression from both sides peaked.

Days before Erdogan's arrival, statements started coming from the Turkish side. "Erdogan will go to Pakistan, he will pull ears," was the rhetoric through different channels. The Pakistani side's silence was due to their busy schedule preparing to deport Turkish educators, as it turned out later.

On Sunday, November 15, 2016, PakTurk Education Foundation management received an official letter from the Ministry of Interior stating that the visas and the residence permits of the Turkish educators would not be extended and that the 108 educators and their family members mentioned in an exhaustive list had to leave Pakistan within three days the latest. The fact such a critical official document was delivered over the weekend showed the Government of Pakistan did not take this decision easily. Dispatched hours before Erdogan's arrival in Pakistan, this communiqué denoted that the visa renewal issue had been kept on hold until the last moment when the Pakistani authorities could no longer resist the pressure from Turkiye. The government officials' silence, especially during the last two months before the deportation notice, and the way they acted as if they had shelved the crisis showed their insincere attitude towards the PakTurk Schools, notwithstanding years of interaction and mutual goodwill. Curious, the Ministry of Interior officials, who kept spelling the names of the PakTurk Schools and the title of the Foundation correctly for 20-odd years, also made glaring typos across the deportation notice. This gave an idea of how hurried the decision might have been dispatched and, as if to confirm the adage "Haste makes waste", brought a catastrophe with this speed.

The Pakistani government's deportation decision was reported as breaking news around the world. Erdogan, who was about to leave Turkiye for Pakistan, spoke to the Turkish press in his departing statement, thanking Pakistan for the 'gesture'. Pro-Erdogan media groups in Turkiye interpreted the deportation order as a gift from the Government of Pakistan to Erdogan in honor of his forthcoming visit. Meanwhile, they chose to ignore the human tragedy and exploited the situation to effervesce their servitude to the regime. They went so vulgar in breaking the news to the Turkish public, welcoming this unprecedented tragic event in the history of both countries with pomp and show.

The ruthless Turkish officials and their bonded associates will be remembered in history as those who usurped or put locks on the gates of the schools opened by their own citizens; the schools that conquered the hearts of people of all faiths on every continent; the schools that stood out as islands of peace worldwide, so to speak, when violence and marginalization were rampant, and the world kept thirsting for acceptance and forbearance; the schools that inspired those who had lost the hope for peaceful coexistence…

Is there any other group in history that has traveled between continents to lock the doors of schools opened by their own people, bribing the host countries with wealth, and declaring war on innocent teachers?

Everyone was shocked. How can you stop life in three days? How can you leave the country where you have spent years, the country you consider your second home, without looking back? Is it so easy to fit decades in a suitcase?

And where to go? The regime in your own country has slandered you a terrorist, you cannot return to your homeland. The country you love, the country you have worked day and night for, ordered you to "leave within three days". Questions, questions...

Leaving thousands of students and thousands of friends behind is the heftiest trial... Stifled by these, words get stuck in your throat and tears well your eyes. Bad news traveled at light speed and students kept crying, parents were devastated. The school buildings and the residences of the teachers overflowed with students, parents, and friends, who tried to understand the situation and support the teachers.

The words fail in those moments. On one side there was a ruthless political mindset who would take your life if they could, and on the other side were parents who offered you money saying, "You are undergoing hard times" and heartfelt friends who tried to hand you the heirlooms they fetched from their homes...

While Ottoman Turkiye was struggling for life and death against the great powers on different fronts, especially since the beginning of the 20th century, Allama Dr. Iqbal addressed a large congregation of Indian Muslims in 1913 in Lahore to appeal to their donations for the Ottoman Turkiye and, people there donated all they had, including their jewelry and life savings, for the national struggle our ancestors upheld back then. It was yesterday once more as our Pakistani brothers and sisters with their children and relatives demonstrated another matchless self-sacrifice and heartfelt concern towards the plight of the Turkish educators in November 2016 and onwards. It was as if history was repeating itself. The nation of Allama Dr. Muhammad Iqbal stood up for the Turkish educators that day too. They were true to the core, contrary to some politicians emotionally(!) attached to the Turkish regime.

It was a time brimming with sincere emotion and concern. The devotion shown by their Pakistani students and the parents will always remain in the memories of Turkish educators as golden moments. Each teacher politely declined the precious and valuable offers made by the students and parents. After all, they had not come to take the gold and wealth of the country, but to set thrones in the hearts and educate bright generations. The educators' stance and kindness even in those days of hardship won the hearts of their Pakistani friends and parents.

While both Erdogan's visit and the imminent deportation of the Turkish educators headlined in the news and TV talk shows, one commentator on a private TV channel made a historical remark: "Several deportations transpired in the history of Pakistan, and the fastest was the deportation of an Indian spy. He was deported within four days. Turks are not our enemies like the Indians; they are a nation we call as our brothers and sisters. These people have been in our country and served in diverse fields for over 20 years. We entrusted our children to them; yet, it is a great shame the sympathy and tolerance shown to an Indian spy has not been shown to the Turkish teachers."

With this ordeal, the Turkish educators of the PakTurk Schools went into history as the first Hizmet Movement volunteers to be victimized by two countries simultaneously. The order from the Government of Pakistan was rigid, "Leave the country!", but where to go? There was absolutely no question of returning to Turkiye. You needed a visa to travel to a third country. While some had visas to other countries, their spouses and children did not. With backs against the wall, everyone sought ways out. Relocating the Turkish educators to countries where no problems existed became the top priority. Moving the courts against the deportation order was an additional option. In an attempt to ensure the educators' smooth exit from Pakistan, extending the stipulated period in consultation with the Government of Pakistan was suggested as the third option. Another option was visiting different embassies in Islamabad and applying for visas.

This smothering experience reminded me of the incident between Prophet Moses (peace be upon him) and the Pharaoh. Prophet Moses (peace be upon him), who set out to save his people from oppression, was pursued by the Pharaoh. The Pharaoh and his army caught up with Prophet Moses and his people near the shore of the Red Sea. In the front was a sea unyielding like the Pharaoh and behind them was the fast-approaching Pharaoh and wave after wave of soldiers. Caught in the middle were Prophet Moses (peace be upon him) and his people. Depleted were the causes and the believers had no means but to surrender themselves to the ocean of trust and resignation in God. Our vulnerability was a projection to that of Prophet Moses and his people when the governments of Turkiye and Pakistan came upon us in tandem; they neither allowed us to remain in Pakistan nor allowed us to return and live in our homeland in safety.

Time was of utmost essence and options were limited. The teachers tuned their hearts to God, the Most Merciful and the All-Seeing of their every condition. While they raced against time to pack their luggage and settle their affairs, they also kept pleading in prayer and supplication with the cry, "O Lord, help us!"

If the other three plans did not materialize, educators without a visa to a third country had two options: Applying for asylum or applying for teaching jobs in countries where they could enter with on-arrival visas. While teachers reviewed options and made attempts, PakTurk educational institutions moved the Islamabad High Court for a stay order on the deportation issue. Having listened to the respective PakTurk official on the courtesy of the situation, the judge said the PakTurk case was a residency issue and it was up to the Ministry of Interior to decide whether to grant a visa or residency permit. The court did not process the case, but advised the PakTurk officials to contact the Ministry of Interior for a time extension. Upon the court's recommendation, the Turkish educators at the PakTurk educational institutions applied to the Ministry of Interior for an extension, on grounds of the implausible duration given for leaving Pakistan. Granting an extension verbally until November 30, 2016, the Ministry of Interior officials rejected issuing an official letter documenting this grace period, despite multiple requests.

The grace period until November 30, 2016 provided the Turkish educators of the PakTurk educational institutions with a new hope and a fresh opportunity to follow solid steps for an urgent solution.

Despite Erdogan's visit, Pakistani media kept discussing the expulsion of the Turkish educators, while regional and international media followed the developments closely to have the latest updates.

Despite severe criticisms against Pakistan in terms of democracy and freedoms, the mobility and autonomy of the media and judicial institutions have been far ahead of Turkiye.

Opinion-makers were not afraid to criticize the government or prosecute corruption, and law enforcement officials could fulfill their jobs to the letter. This was something people longed for under the Erdogan regime.

Turkish educators, who could breathe easier after the Ministry of Interior's extension of the deportation deadline, started packing up their luggage and selling their household items and cars. In Islamabad in particular, dealers who took advantage of the urgent need of several friends to sell their cars, came to the campuses where the vehicles were parked and made throwaway offers to seal the deals in their favor. Opportunists were in action.

There were 28 K-12 PakTurk educational institutions in 10 cities and 4 provinces of Pakistan. After the negative response from the Islamabad High Court for a stay order against deportation, our colleagues in the four provinces contacted their lawyers and prepared official documents to apply to the provincial high courts, requesting a stay of the federal government's decision. The media closely followed the lawsuits and the proceedings.

The first of the lawsuits filed in the Lahore High Court was concluded on November 29, 2016. One day before the expiry of the deadline set by the Ministry of Interior, the Court stayed the government's deportation order. This development was announced as the breaking news not only in the national media, but also by international news organizations like the BBC, Reuters, AFP, and AP.

I was among the batch of educators who met the UNHCR (United Nations High Commissioner for Refugees) officials in Karachi. Aware of the Erdogan regime's rights violations and witch-hunts in Turkiye and worldwide, the UNHCR gave the green light to grant the Turkish educators asylum-seeker certificates against persecution. No doubt, this process was time-consuming and required intensive work to ensure simultaneous progress and delivery in four provinces of Pakistan. The number of Turkish educators, including their family members, was around 450. While applying for the asylum-seeker certificates in Karachi, I witnessed the UNHCR Representation Office cancel the holidays of its staff to ensure the timely process and delivery of the certificates to the Turkish educators. Similarly, the UNHCR offices in Islamabad, Lahore, Peshawar, and Quetta too worked overtime to have the certificates ready before the deportation deadline. Farther than just filling out some forms and submitting a few documents, the asylum certificate applications were fairly detailed with personal interviews, crosschecking the submitted data with the information on the forms, and obtaining the biometrics. Under normal circumstances, it would have taken months to get to the interview phase, but the UNHCR acted swiftly to alleviate the humanitarian tragedy and granted asylum-seeker certificates to all the educators and their families. I believe the decision of the Lahore High Court also influenced the UNHCR's action.

This decision of the UNHCR in Pakistan against Erdogan's "Turkish educators are terrorists" rhetoric served as a reference for several countries worldwide. With the PakTurk teachers under the protection of the United Nations, it was thus stated at the highest level that the Gulen Movement and its activities were not considered as terrorist activities by the United Nations, despite all the smear attempts made by Erdogan and his regime officials immediately after the faux coup.

In the following months, the Sindh and Peshawar High Courts also took the UNHCR decision as a reference and sanctioned the federal government to stop deportations. The high courts in Karachi and Peshawar stated that the Turkish educators would not be subjected to any political or social pressure and would not be deported, contrary to the federal government's pressure. Each province in Pakistan has its own government, chief minister, parliament, and judiciary, just like in the United States. Back then, PML-N, the party that ran the federal government was also in power in the Punjab province with a population of over 130 million. Nawaz Sharif, the occasional Prime Minister and Shehbaz Sharif, the occasional Chief Minister of the Punjab, are brothers. This was why a greater chunk of the trouble in the process transpired in Islamabad, the federal capital, and Lahore, the capital of the Punjab province.

Meanwhile, a colleague contacted the German Consulate in Karachi and was told "We can give visas to your colleagues in need." On November 23, 2016, nearly 30 families (100 people in total) applied for German visas in Karachi. Visa applications were completed in two to three days. I was the last one to apply because I was interpreting for my colleagues. While my application was under process, a Consulate official came, took the basket containing the passports, and left the visa office. When I asked the officer processing the application, he said, "It is a routine procedure. There is no problem" and completed my process.

The visa officer said they would inform us about the result by November 30 at the latest. "Your colleagues can pick up their passports on November 25," said the officer who processed my visa application while another officer had hurriedly taken the passports from the office. Although we were skeptical, my colleagues and I hoped we would be granted visas soon.

On November 25, 2016, four colleagues who had arrived at the German Consulate with high hopes and representing everyone were deeply disappointed when they saw the rejection note stamped on each passport. I can still remember their sadness.

Elated by the Lahore High Court's decision to stop deportation and the UNHCR's announcement that it would step in and grant asylum-seeker certificates, our colleagues were disappointed when their visa applications were rejected by the German Consulate in Karachi.

Meanwhile, we had to set up housing in Pakistan for the second time, thanks to the latest developments telling us we could stay in the country for some time more. Yet, just like me, most colleagues had sold our household items and cars, thinking we would leave urgently.

UNHCR's decision to grant us asylum-seeker certificates and its swift implementation was welcomed by both local and international human rights organizations and institutions, and they shared their satisfaction through various news channels. Pakistan's renowned English daily Dawn, one of the first media outlets to announce UNHCR's decision to Pakistan and the world, came out with the headline "UNHCR Gives Turkish Teachers Protection but No Jobs".

In a succession of events, each one tougher than the last, the PakTurk teachers were granted protection and asylum-seeker certificates by the UNHCR, which enabled them to stay in Pakistan a little longer, but they had lost their legal right to work because their visas had not been extended. This made me and my colleagues very anxious. During the first months, we tried to survive on our personal savings and the limited compensation we received when we were severed from the PakTurk Schools. As a remedy to this unsustainable situation, altruistic and generous philanthropists, who were aware of the events, extended their helping hands to us. This way, our basic problems could partially be solved.

ERDOGAN'S EVENTFUL VISIT TO PAKISTAN

On November 10, 2016, Erdogan's impending visit to Pakistan was confirmed and the Pakistani media intensified their reports on the post-July 15 scenarios in Pakistan and Turkiye. A hot topic on regular circulation for the last three years, PakTurk Schools and their future status were widely discussed in the Pakistani media. The news reports and the commentators dwelt more on the likely impact of Erdogan's visit on the PakTurk Schools.

A week before Erdogan's visit, on November 7-8, 2016, İlnur Çevik, Erdogan's Chief Advisor, visited Pakistan to speak at a conference at the University of Management and Technology in Lahore and wrote a column in Yeni Birlik daily about his observations of the visit. Çevik criticized Pakistan for its 'lenient' approach to the PakTurk Schools. Going even further and using expressions which do not befit diplomatic courtesy, he stated that Erdogan would "need to pull some ears in Pakistan during his visit". Used by a foreign government official for another sovereign country, such words violate the boundaries of diplomatic courtesy and reflects the sickening state of Turkiye's view of Pakistan.

The Turkish government under Erdogan's tutelage did not treat Pakistan with due respect in this process, either through rhetoric or conduct. It was unacceptable for someone at the level of a presidential advisor to insult Pakistan with such statements deliberately styled without diplomatic courtesy.

İlnur Çevik's rash statements caused concern among the PakTurk officials. An intensive and stressful 20-day period preceded Erdogan's official visit to Pakistan.

Having been informed of the impending deportation of the Turkish educators, Erdogan thanked the Pakistani authorities as he boarded his plane bound for Pakistan on November 15, 2016. Prime Minister Nawaz Sharif and his brother Punjab Chief Minister Shehbaz Sharif, Prime Minister of Pakistan as of July 2023, welcomed their 'bosom friend' President Erdogan enthusiastically with a high-level reception at the Chaklala Air Base in Rawalpindi.

The Turkish media saw the Pakistani government's decision to expel the Turkish educators just before Erdogan's visit as a gift from Pakistan to him.

There was also a surprise development during Erdogan's visit. The opposition party Pakistan Tehreek-e-Insaaf (PTI) led by Imran Khan boycotted the plenary session of the National Assembly of Pakistan held in honor of Erdogan. Imran Khan's boycott of the plenary session of the parliament, where "an important state guest was to address the Pakistani parliamentarians", dropped a bombshell on the agenda. When Imran Khan offered to meet Erdogan separately, this time Erdogan rejected him saying "He would not meet because he and his party did not attend the joint parliamentary session". This first made me think that Imran Khan, who kept looking for opportunities to erode the Nawaz Sharif government especially by criticizing the Sharif family's intimacy with the Erdogan family, refused to listen to Erdogan's speech in the parliament, gained a principled edge for his party. Later, it turned out I had been wrong. Imran Khan boycotted the parliamentary session not because of the anomalous business and social relations between the Sharif family and the Erdogan family, but simply to make nuisance for the incumbent government and oppose for mere opposition. After Imran Khan's declaration of parliamentary session boycott which jeopardized Erdogan's address to a "united National Assembly of Pakistan", the Turkish Embassy Islamabad contacted Imran Khan's party officials to convince Imran Khan and the PTI parliamentarians to attend Erdogan's speech, but failed. The Embassy's insistent efforts for shuttling between the parties to urgently resolve the problem signaled Ankara's, and especially Erdogan's, discomfort with the potential fallouts of the boycott.

Erdogan's address to the joint session of the National Assembly of Pakistan garnered much media attention. The speech was also broadcast live in Turkiye. Anadolu Agency, covering Erdogan's speech in the parliament which received the intense applause of the Pakistani deputies, added the following on social media: "Surprise for Erdogan from the

Pakistani Parliament! All deputies in the parliament stood up and welcomed Erdogan by thumping their desks, signaling support in Pakistan."

Making an extensive speech in the National Assembly of Pakistan, Erdogan actionated and, leaving the issues of bilateral relations aside, plunged head-first to denigrate the Hizmet Movement. He said, "They say they follow interfaith dialogue in the West... What's dialogue? Can there be such a thing in Islam?" and strove to manage the perceptions of the members of the Pakistani Parliament. It is rather significant how Erdogan uses differing discourses in Western countries and Muslim countries. His turns, lies, and manipulations in Turkiye have been known to everyone. Can a tiger change its stripes? He assumed this crooked conduct abroad as well. While he could effortlessly say, "What's interfaith dialogue? It has no place in Islam" in Pakistan, in the West he took pride in establishing dialogue platforms like the Alliance of Civilizations with Spain at the level of heads of state on his own initiative. In the West, he could socialize with leaders on the grounds of intercultural and interfaith dialogue. In short, Erdogan kept marketing his assorted versions in the West and in the East.

An interesting aspect of this official visit was the sumptuous banquet hosted by the Punjab Chief Minister Shehbaz Sharif in honor of Erdogan in Lahore. Dedicating one day of the two-day official visit to sightseeing and a dinner program in Lahore was criticized in the media, with the comment that the relationship between Turkiye and Pakistan was shadowed by the personal relationship between the Sharif family and the Erdogan family.

A Pakistani journalist rightly asked in his column, "What does Pakistan get from Erdogan's visit? Is it just the promised state scholarships for 250 Ph.D. students?" The journalist wrote the pomp and circumstance of Erdogan's visit was only a show and had no lasting benefits for either country. As planned, Erdogan traveled from Islamabad to Lahore and spent a full day of his two-day official visit there for a lavish welcome and dinner.

Events unfolded to the detriment of the PakTurk Schools, and the institutions were inflicted with bad publicity through the efforts of both governments. The Erdogan regime was on cloud nine. Still, Erdogan was annoyed with the failure in having the PakTurk Schools transferred to the Maarif Foundation simultaneously with the expulsion decision, and with the failure of the Pakistani authorities, whom he considered as his vassals. He urged the Pakistani officials to urgently resolve the PakTurk Schools' transfer issue.

Around this time, the Pakistani government officials, tired of the unrelenting pressure, asked the Turkish officials, "You talk about an organization called the Maarif Foundation, but this structure does not exist here. Even if there is, how will this work be done?" Almost immediately, the Turkiye Maarif Foundation (TMF) was mobilized and a representation office was opened in Islamabad within days before Erdogan's November 2016 visit by securing a 'provisional' international NGO registration from the Ministry of Interior despite its governmental nature and through bypassing all protocols which otherwise require months-long security and official clearances.

TURKIYE MAARIF FOUNDATION ARRIVES IN PAKISTAN

Erdogan's entourage included ministers, businessmen, and chief executives of the Turkiye Maarif Foundation. Several TMF officials had arrived in Pakistan days before and started the preliminary procedures for transferring the PakTurk Schools.

Erdogan wanted the transfer of the schools to the TMF immediately, preferably through a ceremony he would preside, showing in every gesture that this has been a personal obsession. The PakTurk Schools' campuses and the number of students whetted his appetite. He did not hesitate to use Pakistan for his own political ambitions. The success of the Hizmet Movement in Turkiye and worldwide disturbed him, and he showed the whole world the extent of his hatred and envy against the Hizmet institutions.

On November 16, 2016, Pakistan did not respond positively to Erdogan, who wished the transfer concluded during his short visit, and expected him to be satisfied with the deportation order.

LIKELY REASONS FOR NOT TRANSFERRING THE SCHOOLS IMMEDIATELY AFTER THE DEPORTATION VERDICT

❖ Much talked about in media, the government officials feared a backlash from the public who had been vocal against a foreign government's intervention to a deep-seated local private chain of schools. The officials also feared the issue could snowball with unsought consequences.

❖ The ongoing hearings in the Supreme Court of Pakistan Court on corruption charges against them had worn the Sharif family down, and they did not want to open another front for themselves by risking the possibility of going to court on this issue as well.

❖ Due to the lack of legal grounds for the seizure or transfer of the PakTurk Schools and the fact that PakTurk Education Foundation was a certified local foundation, the officials may have wanted to spread this issue over time.

❖ The Pakistani government too had its own demands from the Turkish government that were not covered in the media. It was rumored that the officials kept waiting for Turkiye to address these demands and did not want to lose their advantage immediately. For instance, it was alleged that the Pakistani officials might have kept the PakTurk Schools case as a bargaining chip for the erstwhile international arbitration litigation between the Karkey Karadeniz Elektrik power generation company and the Government of Pakistan and the huge compensation Pakistan was likely to pay. It is still unclear.

It showed Erdogan had made a special request to the Pakistani authorities to register the Turkiye Maarif Foundation in Pakistan immediately. During Erdogan's visit, the TMF President and the then-Federal Minister of Education Muhammad Baligh-ur-Rahman – who was also a parent of the school where I worked – held an official meeting and signed an agreement for the TMF to carry out educational activities in Pakistan.

I was in frequent contact with the Federal Minister of Education because his children were studying at my school. Despite the crises and allegations, the Minister continued to send his children to our school, giving the impression that he had a different view from his political party. On May 20, 2016, I accompanied three students including the Minister's daughter in grade 8 to the Model UN Conference held at the United Nations headquarters in Geneva, Switzerland, as the team coordinator. When I shared with him the video and photos of his daughter's speech during the program, he texted me, "The Hizmet Movement has been a source of light for South Asia with its educational activities. I thank you for your work." His late wife, Mrs. Uzma, did not refrain from meeting with us even after November 2016 and came to my house for iftar with her children during Ramadan 2017.

Before Erdogan's visit, PakTurk officials had visited the Minister at the Federal Ministry of Education. When they asked him about his view about the media-assisted allegations from Turkiye, he said "Don't be afraid". Unfortunately, he himself signed the agreement with the TMF officials and sealed the fate of PakTurk Schools without hesitation.

With the signing of the protocol, the TMF applied to the Securities & Exchange Commission (SECP) for its official registration. Shehbaz Sharif, who wanted the registration completed immediately, did not hesitate to order the senior officials to have this done within a day. He gave special orders to the respective SECP officers not to leave, no matter what time it was, until the registration was completed... and as expected, the process that would have taken months was completed in one day.

Although the TMF was established under the auspices of the Erdogan regime as a shadow Ministry of National Education with state funds, it was registered as an international NGO with the SECP and Ministry of Interior in Pakistan, through the Turkish Embassy in Islamabad. This means that the foundation, which the Erdogan regime calls a public institution in Turkiye and pours millions of dollars from the Treasury Department, more precisely the amount earmarked from the Ministry of National Education and the discretionary funds released via frequent executive orders, operates abroad as a subcontractor entity. The manner of registration is a matter of debate.

Hürriyet columnist Vahap Munyar, who stayed at the Serena Hotel Islamabad where Erdogan stayed during his official visit, wrote in detail about the TMF's strategy after the deportation decision against the Turkish educators in his column:

As we were having tea after dinner at the Serena Hotel where we were staying, the Education Attaché of the Turkish Embassy Islamabad and the Pakistan Representative of the Maarif Foundation came to our table and the discussion took a turn towards the PakTurk Schools:

- Government of Pakistan seized the company called Pak-Turk which runs 28 schools. The decision for deporting 108 teachers working in these schools was also announced as a gesture a day before our President's visit.

The representative of the Maarif Foundation showed me the file in his hand:

- As the TMF, we signed a preliminary agreement with the Government of Pakistan to open and operate schools across the country. This agreement paved the way for us to manage the Pak-Turk Schools.

He emphasized that over 10,000 students were studying in 28 schools:

- Education continues in the schools. As the TMF, we brought 120 teachers from Turkiye to Pakistan. Local teachers are already working in the schools.

He explained the formula for taking over the management of the Pak-Turk Schools:

- I will enter the management of the Pak-Turk as the TMF representative. The Government of Pakistan has opened this door for us and our role in the management will increase over time.

It was a sign that the TMF's plan to take over the PakTurk schools, which journalist Munyar mentioned in his column, was in full swing as of November 17, 2016. Both the Turkish Embassy Islamabad and the TMF executives were persistently pursuing the matter of taking over the PakTurk Schools, a manifestation of Erdogan's personal ambition.

The details Munyar mentioned specifically refer to the attempts to take over the school management with intrigues. As PakTurk management realized the sinister developments, they moved the Labor Court and prevented these efforts.

As Munyar also mentioned in his article, although the TMF was not yet certified and a decision about the schools were yet to be finalized, Erdogan's delegation included TMF teachers flown in from Turkiye. These teachers were enrolled in a basic-level English course at the National University of Modern Languages (NUML) in Islamabad. With teachers not proficient in English, the TMF was planning to take over the schools. This issue alone was enough to show the damage intended for the institutions.

The new teachers brought in by the TMF were blatant fans of Erdogan, defending political Islamist views and Erdogan as the leader of the Muslim world through photos and posts on their social media profiles. They had no qualms about working in privately-owned schools illegally seized.

Given the teachers with the mentioned vision and mission, it was clear to what mindset the PakTurk institutions were planned to be transferred. By lowering the level of education in the schools, not only Turkiye would suffer a loss of reputation, but also the educational institutions which led Pakistan from success to success would be dealt a blow. It was also clear from the social media profiles of the proposed teachers that the schools would be used for Erdogan propaganda.

Such an infiltration to the educational system would not only cause discomfort for students and parents, but also mean the indoctrination of a generation with detrimental politics.

No.6/7/2010-P.E-III
GOVERNMENT OF PAKISTAN
MINISTRY OF INTERIOR
◇◇◇◇

Islamabad, the 11th November, 2016

From: Muhammad Hafeez,
          Section Officer (PE-III)
          Tel: 051-9207494

To:

          CEO,
          M/S. PakTurk International Cag Education Foundation
          Plot No. 87 & 88, Faiz Ahmad Faiz Road,
          Sector H-8/1,
          Islamabad.

Subject: **VISA EXTENSION CASES – PAK-TURK EDUCAITON FOUNDATION
          AND PAK-TURK INTERNATIONAL CAG EDUCATION FOUNDATION**

          Reference your request regarding extension in visas of administrative and
teaching staff alongwith family members of M/S. Pak-Turk Education Foundation & M/S. Pak-
Turk International Cag Education Foundation in Pakistan (List enclosed).

2.   Your request has been considered at appropriate level but it has not been
acceded to.

(Muhammad Hafeez)
Section Officer (PE-III)

No. 6/7/2010-P.E (III)
GOVERNMENT OF PAKISTAN
MINISTRY OF INTERIOR

Islamabad, the 14th November, 2016

To:

1.   Deputy Director (Immigration),Federal Investigation Agency (FIA),
     Benazir Bhutto International Airport
     ISLAMABAD

2.   Deputy Director (Immigration),Federal Investigation Agency (FIA),
     Jinnah International Airport,
     KARACHI

3.   Deputy Director (Immigration),Federal Investigation Agency (FIA),
     Allama Iqbal International Airport,
     Lahore

4.   Deputy Director (Immigration), Federal Investigation Agency (FIA)
     Bacha Khan International Airport,
     Peshawar.

5.   Deputy Director (Immigration), Federal Investigation Agency (FIA)
     International Airport,
     Quetta.

Subject: **EXIT PERMIT**

          This Ministry has agreed to allow exit from Pakistan to the foreign nationals in the
attached list if not borne on Blacklist/ECL.

2.   The foreigners are directed to exit from Pakistan before 20th November, 2016,
positively, without payment of overstay charges, on the authority of this permission from any
International Airport of Pakistan.

(Muhammad Hafeez)
Section Officer (PE-III)

Copy to:-

          M/S Pak Turk International Cag Education Foundation, Islamabad.

Section Officer (PE-III)

*The deportation letter, along with a list containing approximately
450 Turkish nationals, was dispatched to the PakTurk Education
Central Office on November 15th, 2016 just a day before
Erdogan's visit to Pakistan.*

Chapter 4

Tribulations in a Foreign Land

(November 16, 2016 –
September 27, 2017)

This section explains the developments after the deportation order issued against the Turkish educators and the fourth phase of the escalating crisis.

The details of the deportation order affecting nearly 450 people including 108 Turkish educators and their families, and the repercussions of Erdogan's official visit to Pakistan in November 2016 were explained in Chapter 3.

Notwithstanding the deportation order against the Turkish educators, PakTurk Schools continued their educational activities without interruption. PakTurk management informed the Pakistani teachers and staff that handing over the schools to another entity was out of question and that the Pakistani teachers were in complete charge of the schools' activities.

The key reason education continued uninterrupted despite crises was the PakTurk administration's decision to appoint Pakistani principals to the PakTurk Schools on August 10, 2016. The wisdom behind this action became evident much later. For about three months until November 16, 2016 when all hell broke loose, the Pakistani administrators who had worked with their Turkish counterparts responded to the crisis so swiftly and prudently and contributed to the smooth running of the PakTurk Schools.

Parent representatives and the alumni had reacted to the deportation of the Turkish educators with press statements, calling on the Government of Pakistan to reverse its decision. The Turkish educators applied to the respective authorities in every city where the PakTurk Schools were located to have their visas and residence permits extended and the press conferences they held were widely covered in the press.

In addition to the decisions of the Lahore, Sindh, and Peshawar High Courts and the federal government suspending deportation, the protection through the asylum-seeker certificates granted by the UNHCR gave the Turkish educators much-needed relief and time to prepare more conveniently.

Having sold their household items and furniture, many colleagues set up homes again thanks to the latest positive developments.

For almost a month from November 22, 2016, I was in Karachi during the process of visa application at the German Consulate. Like other colleagues, I too stayed at a friend's house. Despite all the hardships we experienced during that phase, colleagues showed so sincere and sturdy solidarity with one another. Throughout that period, our friends in Karachi not only opened their homes but also their hearts to us.

The UNHCR officials had told us that the procedure would continue after the issuance of the asylum-seeker certificates, and everyone would be resettled to a third country in safety within three or four years. They said the prolonged timeframe was due to the priority resettlement of the Afghan asylum seekers in Pakistan.

In the wake of the Russian invasion of Afghanistan in December 1979, millions of Afghan refugees arrived in Pakistan. During the 44 years of this crisis, almost two generations of Afghans have grown up and found jobs in Pakistan. Before the arrival of Syrian refugees in Turkiye, Pakistan held the world title for hosting the largest number of refugees. Having not ratified the 1951 and 1967 UN agreements, Pakistan opened its borders to the Afghan nationals and received them as "guests" without citizenship rights and free travel. Afghan refugees were accommodated in refugee camps for years and were not allowed to leave their assigned districts.

In November 2016, when the Turkish educators received the deportation order, nearly 350,000 Afghan refugees were registered with the UNHCR offices in Pakistan. They kept waiting for the UNHCR to resettle them in a third country or repatriate them to Afghanistan safely. The UNHCR officials told us they would not expedite the process for the Turkish educators. This meant a wait of at least three or four years.

This being the case, my colleagues and I rented houses and bought furniture for the second time. We returned from Karachi, rented a house in an affordable neighborhood in Islamabad and modestly set my house from scratch.

All colleagues who were to live in Pakistan for at least another year rented houses and tried to settle down after an earth-shaking experience. Our students and parents were so happy about the latest developments and hoped the government would soon make a decision in our favor.

TEACHERS' SMALL AND MODEST HOMES

Despite their limited means, the Turkish teachers kept hosting guests from all walks of life in their new homes and showed people the beauty of the cause they represented under all circumstances. This time too, those modest houses were distinguished as places of sublime service notwithstanding the difficult conditions.

The Turkish teachers, who have always been committed to living frugally and saving, did not compromise on self-sacrifice for their students during this period. They mobilized all their means to stay in touch with them. During this troubled period, parents and students would visit our homes for iftar dinners and enjoy the blessings of Ramadan with us.

WREATHED SORROWS: WHILE IN PAKISTAN, TEACHERS LOSE PARENTS IN TURKIYE

On the one hand were the intrigues played on the PakTurk Schools. On the other hand were the troubles our colleagues suffered due to an uncertain future. Despite everything, Turkish educators faced the events with patience and perseverance. Amidst the turmoil in Pakistan where they kept encountering developments which they would not even dream of in their lives, three colleagues sank in further sadness when they learned of the demise of their loved ones.

The events kept speaking to us through their own tongue and accent, but we were yet to comprehend them. Everyone felt the blow of the developments, and whatever befell the Turkish educators in Pakistan was reflected on their families in Turkiye. Friends who lost their parents could not even visit Turkiye to attend their funerals. Trying our best to soothe the pang of separation, we occasionally came together and offered funeral prayers in absentia. We prayed and did our best to share the pain of our colleagues.

I received the news of my mother's death in 2018. Unfortunately, I could not attend her funeral in my hometown. My mother departed to the eternal world, and

I could not recite a prayer at her graveside. The news of her passing also saddened my friends. When I lost my mother, I felt the helpless feelings of my colleagues abroad who lost their parents back home. The hard feeling of being abroad and not having a secure passage to visit my country and fulfill my last duties to my mother made me understand the extent of their pain.

'STATELESS' BABIES

As of July 20, 2016 and in violation of basic citizenship rights, the Turkish Embassy in Islamabad and the Turkish Consulate General in Karachi started to reject processing the applications made by the Turkish educators working in PakTurk Schools. This discriminatory and exclusionary attitude affected everyone in various ways, especially the parents of the newborn babies. Consular officials refused to issue passports and ID cards to the babies.

Some colleagues visited the Embassy and Consulate General and told the officials that their children are entitled to the national ID cards and passports as their constitutional right, but they were refused. When they cautioned officials, "What you are doing is a constitutional crime," they were told, "There are strict orders from Ankara, we cannot issue any document to you."

The innocent babies subjected to discrimination soon after they opened their eyes to the world were not aware of the decision their home country's government had taken against them, but their parents were devastated by the discrimination meted out of to their innocent children.

UNIVERSITY-AGE YOUTH

The university-age children of our colleagues could not get visas from the embassies of the countries where their universities were located. They could not send documents requested by the institutions because the Turkish Embassy in Islamabad or the Turkish Consulate General in Karachi did not provide them, and their applications were rejected because they did not have residency in Pakistan or elsewhere.

In several cases, the high-school children of the Turkish educators were refused admission to the SAT exam venues by the invigilators because of their expired passports. The local exam authorities, who required valid passports for identity checks, did not take the students' applications into account.

With their conditions getting tougher on each day, victimized teachers' room for maneuver kept shrinking.

TEACHER SUFFERS HEART ATTACK

Despite all unfavorable conditions, everyone worked hard for the educational institutions built brick by brick with the countless efforts, sweat, and tears of thousands of self-sacrificing people. A perpetual struggle was underway to prevent the PakTurk Schools from falling into the hands of usurpers.

On April 21, 2017, everyone was saddened to learn about the arrest of a colleague in Turkiye. Mr. Mehmet Ali Şeker, one of our colleagues in Lahore, suffered a heart attack that night. Thanks to the timely intervention, Mr. Şeker was saved at the hospital. Mr. Mehmet's heart attack saddened everyone and affected morales. Nevertheless, we were all happy and grateful that he survived.

BROKEN HEARTS

In an interview with journalist Ahmet Dönmez, teacher Ali Yılmaz said, "My heart is broken. I cannot accept they treat us as if we are terrorists. We have been serving in Pakistan for so long and have not been fined even a traffic ticket in all these years."

How difficult it was to find someone to commiserate with and tell the truth when people were prone to slander and believed the lies they heard rather than what they saw.

... AND LITTLE CHILDREN

Children were the most affected. While the very young had no awareness of the stifling conditions, the school-going children were burdened with substantial stress.

The parents heartbroken by their children's sadness when they could not afford to buy them even a toy caused me a lot of grief too. I always wished I could bring smiles to their faces with toys and gifts.

UNHCR AT TURKISH EMBASSY'S CROSSHAIRS

While the Turkish educators kept struggling against myriad financial and social hardships which seemed beyond human capacity at times, the Turkish Embassy in Islamabad, obliged by default to resolve the matters of the Turkish citizens, was involved in deeds recorded rare in history. The diplomats worked round the clock to defame their fellow citizens duly representing Turkiye through the tongue of education in Pakistan for years.

The UNHCR-issued asylum-seeker certificates upset the Turkish government, which made them realize they needed to have "the swiftest method to have the Turkish educators expelled out of Pakistan immediately".

Hosting the largest number of refugees in the world, Turkiye meant much for the UNHCR. The Erdogan regime used this edge to threaten the United Nations with the Syrian refugees in Turkiye and even went the distance to accuse the United Nations of supporting terrorists (!).

With the Turkish educators remaining in Pakistan and the PakTurk Schools not handed over to the TMF, the Turkish Embassy in Islamabad was infuriated and became even more aggressive. As if all the oppression and persecution they inflicted by forcing the Government of Pakistan were not enough, the Turkish Embassy made a full court press on the Pakistani media and hosted several Pakistani journalists on information tours to Turkiye by deploying lavish means of the state, and cajoled the journalists to report against the PakTurk Schools and the Turkish educators. Meanwhile, the diplomats and the contract staff at the Turkish Embassy in Islamabad visited public institutions, think-tanks, businesses, and prominent personalities, applying pressure, spreading disinformation, and demanding the Government of Pakistan to take urgent decisions to fulfill the demands.

The UNHCR's granting protection and asylum certificates

to the Turkish educators, despite knowing Turkiye's political sensitivities and the fact Turkiye opened its doors over 3.5 million Syrian refugees, was both pleasing and democratic for the educators. The UNHCR doing its best to prevent a humanitarian tragedy during the PakTurk crisis and taking a decision that drew flak from both Turkiye and Pakistan denoted that humanity was not dead.

Later, in a meeting at the UNHCR, a UNHCR official told our colleague representing the Turkish educators, "You defy the usual refugee profile we see in several crises worldwide. You are a group of highly educated people with an open worldview. This situation you are in is rather saddening." Supporting the Turkish educators throughout the process, the UNHCR case officers gave their numbers to everyone who wished to reach them 7/24 in case of any problem.

TURKISH EMBASSY ENGAGED IN DIRTY FIGHT

At the beginning of 2017, the Turkish Embassy in Islamabad started to spread disinformation all over Pakistan through the local and Turkish media. Including the news about the dastardly July 15 coup conspiracy, the Embassy officials ensured the disinformation about the Hizmet Movement, Fethullah Gulen, PakTurk Schools, etc. which appeared in the regime-tutored media in Turkiye, appeared verbatim in the Pakistani media. They even deployed local and Turkish hired pens to write articles and produce content.

The most outrageous incident was the Turkish Embassy's distribution of magazines and pamphlets to guests at a reception on the anniversary of the July 15 coup conspiracy, containing unsubstantiated and fabricated allegations by the Turkish government. The distribution of the pamphlets to guests, media, and government offices caused us serious concern.

We acted against the Turkish Embassy's dirty information war to shield the teachers and institutions in Pakistan against harassment. With our friends, we kept sharing the updates and analyses in the international media and social media with state institutions, local media, and personalities to provide accurate information against this smear campaign.

The Turkish Embassy's unwarranted attempt to spread false news was thwarted with great effort. Unable to get what they wanted, such as the summary expulsion of the Turkish teachers and transferring the PakTurk Schools, the Embassy was further infuriated.

Seeing that the intrigues were not working, the Turkish Embassy Islamabad took new actions to achieve its goal, this time through unofficial means.

Banking on the Chief Minister Punjab Shehbaz Sharif's good rapport with Erdogan, the Turkish ambassador met the Chief Minister and took a team of the Punjab Police's Counter-Terrorism Department on an information tour to Turkiye in the wake of the July 2016 coup attempt. Indoctrinated and much complimented on this state-sponsored tour, the Pakistani law enforcement delegation was given presentations based on slander and lies. The team returned home laden with the information and equipment the Turkish government desired. We could inadvertently learn about the nature of this trip from Mr. Zekeriya Özşahin, the school principal who was forcibly taken from his home in Islamabad soon after the abduction of the Kaçmaz family in Lahore, arrested, beaten, and physically tortured at a police station. The Pakistani law enforcement officers, who treated him with violence and insults also said, "We know you people so well," and after making unspeakable remarks about Fethullah Gulen, they said, "They told us everything about you in Turkiye." It was also revealed that the decision to abduct Turkish educators, especially the Kaçmaz and Ervan families, from Pakistan through intelligence operations was taken during this tour in June 2017.

A DRAFT LAW, COVERTLY RUSHED

While Turkiye kept pressing Pakistan to hand over the PakTurk Schools to the Maarif Foundation, it also provided tactics on how this could be achieved. The PakTurk educational institutions were owned by a local foundation and this had cornered the Pakistani government officials on the principle of abiding by the legal framework and discouraged them from taking any illegal steps. The so-called saving prescription came to Pakistan from Turkiye: "Make an amendment in the Companies Act with the following wording: 'The assets of any organization or foundation found to have committed a crime in a friendly and brotherly country can be confiscated and the said assets can be handed over to different institutions and organizations or foundations." The Nawaz Sharif government, which furtively planned to enact this amendment in February 2017 in an omnibus bill, first withdrew it after the media coverage of the incident, and then shelved it "indefinitely" – until its unofficial use during the phase of transferring the PakTurk Schools to the TMF – after the opposition protested.

MYSTERIOUS AIRCRAFT

A large airliner with a few passengers took off from Turkiye and landed at the Islamabad International Airport. This plane, not a charter flight and with no in-advance arrival details, attracted the attention of an official working at the airport, a relative of a student attending the PakTurk Schools. According to what he learned from the Airport Security Force (ASF), the aircraft had arrived with two MIT (Turkish National Intelligence Organization) officers and about 20 Turkish national police officers with the purpose of "launching a search-and-seizure operation against wanted human traffickers in and around Peshawar". It was soon revealed that the real purpose of the Turkish officials on the plane was to take three Turkish former executives of the PakTurk Schools from Islamabad to Turkiye and that "they had informed the authorities beforehand and so needed no permission for this".

The Turkish Ministry of Interior, which contacted the Pakistani Embassy in Ankara to obtain permission to fly to Pakistan, used the abovementioned pretext of "a joint cross-border operation against human traffickers in Peshawar and its vicinity". This way, the plane landed in Islamabad and the Turkish intelligence and law enforcement officers explained to the Pakistani Federal Ministry of Interior officials that "their intention was not to go to Peshawar, but to collect Turkish educators according to a list". When this was conveyed to the then-Interior Minister Chaudhry Nisar

Ali Khan, he ordered the plane to be flown to Lahore. The plane landed in Lahore and thus attracted the attention of the PakTurk student's relative. Although he did not know of the matter and purely as a joke, he phoned a Turkish teacher he knew and in mid-conversation he quipped, "Good news! We have guests from your country here!" When the PakTurk executives contacted an official from the Federal Ministry of Interior, he confirmed the plane and that it arrived for operational purposes. He said a decision on the plane and its reason for the visit would be made after a meeting at the Interior Ministry. This news caused considerable alarm among the Turkish teachers in Lahore and other cities. Following the meeting, which lasted for several hours and was attended not only by civilian but also military officials, the Federal Ministry of Interior officials expressed their diplomatic disapproval of "the unwarranted visit and its purpose" and described it as "degrading", sharing the view that the Turkish authorities would not allow a similar "operation" on Turkish soil in a similar context. Federal Ministry of Interior and adjoining civilian and military intelligence agencies strongly rejected this "insulting" Turkish "faux pas" and ordered the immediate deportation of the Turkish intelligence and law enforcement officers from Pakistan. Following this incident, Pakistan's Ministry of Foreign Affairs, based on the opinions of the country's respective civilian and military intelligence agencies and the Federal Ministry of Interior, issued a diplomatic note to Turkiye addressed to the then-Turkish Ambassador in Islamabad, Sadık Babür Girgin, stating that "since the documents presented to them by the Turkish authorities regarding the Turkish teachers and the PakTurk educational institutions have been found to be forged and contain false information, the mutual information sharing and security agreements with Turkiye would be suspended in recurrence of a similar incident."

Chaudhry Nisar Ali Khan, lauded as a righteous politician with his stance in Nawaz Sharif's PML-N with his credence in the party and his rejection of illegal practices, had announced on July 27, 2017, two months before the abduction of the Kaçmaz family that he was considering stepping down as Interior Minister and resigning from membership in the National Assembly because of his differences with the party leaders. A day later, on July 28, 2017, the federal cabinet was disbanded following the resignation of Nawaz Sharif after the Panama Papers case decision. Chaudhry Nisar Ali Khan announced that he would not become part of the next federal cabinet of the incoming prime minister Shahid Khaqan Abbasi, who was junior to him. He was replaced by Ahsan Iqbal Chaudhary, a mild-mannered politician who would not raise his voice against the party discourse.

In 2017, a few days before Ramadan, a Pakistani employee of PakTurk Education Foundation was called by one of his friends to a private hospital in Islamabad. When he went to the meeting place, he saw two men next to his friend, who said they worked at the Turkish Embassy in Islamabad and continued: "Don't be afraid of us, we are the representatives of Tayyip Erdogan. We want you to give us the addresses of Murat Ervan's and other PakTurk executives' houses. We will take action against these people after Ramadan." The PakTurk employee, who initially thought not to tell anyone about this incident to avoid getting into trouble, told the details of this meeting to the PakTurk executives concerned, as he had never been harmed by the Turkish executives and his conscience prevailed. When the Turkish executives contacted their lawyers about the matter, they said the "forthcoming act" described by the persons who met the PakTurk employee in the hospital could be done only legally in line with the extradition treaties and similar agreements and that it would be appropriate to take precautions. The UNHCR officials assured the PakTurk officials that there was no need to worry and that the persons under the UN protection could not be subjected to such coercive treatment.

HIGH-FREQUENCY VISITS TO TURKIYE

On February 25, 2017, Punjab Chief Minister Shehbaz Sharif visited Turkiye and met with President Erdogan and Prime Minister Binali Yildirim. Agreements were signed to strengthen relations in several fields.

On March 29, 2017, the Speaker of the Pakistan National Assembly visited Turkiye and met with Erdogan.

On June 21, 2017, Pakistan's Chief of General Staff visited Turkiye and was first received by Erdogan. Later, he met with Fikri Işık, the then-defense minister.

On September 12, 2017, Pakistani Foreign Minister Khawaja Asif visited Turkiye and met with Erdogan.

On September 16, 2017, Punjab Chief Minister Shehbaz Sharif visited Turkiye and met with Erdogan.

These are the recorded high-level visits. Intense high visits before the abduction of the Kaçmaz family on September 27, 2017 showed the games Erdogan kept playing on Pakistan.

As it turned out, Shehbaz Sharif had discussed in detail the plans for the abduction in Pakistan and its consequences. As revealed later, the Nawaz Sharif government did not hesitate to yield to the perpetration of an international crime.

Chapter 5

Abduction of the Kaçmaz Family
and the Aftermath

(September 27, 2017 –
July 4, 2018)

CHRONICLE OF EVENTS: ORDEALS OF THE KAÇMAZ FAMILY AND TURKISH EDUCATORS

The Pakistani state started harassing our friends in Islamabad and Lahore, especially in early September 2017. Our friends in Sindh province and Peshawar faced no visible pressure.

The frequent visits of the Pakistani officials to Turkiye and the growing rapprochement between the two states at all levels had raised concerns among our colleagues. Police and intelligence officers in plainclothes were stationed at the entrances and exits of the streets where the Turkish educators lived and kept them under surveillance in various guises such as electricity or gas meter reader, postman, courier, peddler, or taxi driver. Shopkeepers in the neighborhoods were asked about the arrival and departure times and the routines of the Turkish educators. The sudden increase in the frequency of "inspections" made at teachers' homes by people claiming to be the police or the intelligence raised suspicion. Whenever asked about the reason, these people would reply, "It's all routine, we must check whether you stay at the addresses given to us."

The Kaçmaz family[1] had been aware that they had been under surveillance for days before their house was raided past midnight. They thought there was nothing much to panic about as other teachers' houses too were surveilled.

---

1   Mesut Kaçmaz graduated from the Department of Urdu Language and Literature, Selçuk University, Konya. He is married to Meral Kaçmaz. In 2007, he came to Pakistan and worked as a teacher and school principal until the fateful event when he, his wife Meral Kaçmaz and their daughters Hüda Nur and Hüma Nur were abducted from their home in Lahore at midnight on September 26-27, 2017.

In light of the statements from the neighbors and the house owner, it was later revealed that the operatives shadowing the Kaçmaz family had been preparing for an operation. It was also discovered that when the operatives checked the family's residence in a housing complex in Lahore, they noticed the cameras on various points and they had the footage deleted from these immediately after the abduction. This showed that the intensive visits to the homes of the teachers in Islamabad had not been routine; they had been deliberately carried out to create a distraction before the abduction in Lahore.

At midnight connecting September 26 to 27, 15-20 intelligence or counter-terrorism department officers, who we later learned were men and women in civilian clothes, raided the Kaçmaz family's house on the second floor of a bungalow and forced the family to open the door. When they entered the house, they hustled Mr. and Mrs. Kaçmaz with their daughters. When their upstairs neighbor Fatih Avcu, a former PakTurk teacher, was awakened to the shouting and noises, witnessed the abduction of the family, and intervened with the operatives, he too was taken along with the Kaçmaz family to an undisclosed location.

The Kaçmaz family was abducted as blindfolded and hooded at around 2 a.m. from their home in a central neighborhood of Lahore, the capital of the Punjab province. The person who received the Kaçmaz family and Mr. Fatih where they were taken and who was believed to have directed the operation noticed Mr. Fatih and asked why he had been brought. He looked at a list and said, "This one's name is not here, so let him go." Mr. Fatih was blindfolded and left at a place 15 minutes' walk from his house. Mr. Fatih, who could not even wear his slippers when the incident had taken place, returned home barefoot. This dastardly incident was first heard among the PakTurk teachers and their families in Lahore. Immediately, their colleagues and former PakTurk administrators in Islamabad were informed.

After a brief description of the abduction, I would like to elaborate on the details of the incident:

September 27, 2017

Witness Fatih Avcu: The family was abducted with sacks over their heads

Hearing the news, friends gathered in front of Mr. Mesut Kaçmaz's house and wondered where he and his family might have been taken. Immediately after the incident, the colleagues asked for help from the civil authorities they knew. Learning about the incident, the authorities expressed their surprise and said they would look into the matter.

When the morning dawned in Lahore and the public offices opened, the colleagues visited the police station nearest to where the Kaçmaz family had resided. They demanded to file a first incident report (FIR) on the matter. At first, the officers tried to understand. After talking to a few official authorities about this situation, which seemed strange to them as well, their attitude changed. They said they would not register a case and issue an FIR. No matter how much our colleagues insisted, the police rejected dealing with the matter. Angered by our colleagues' insistence, the police closed the doors in their faces and kicked them out of the police station.

In Islamabad, government and law enforcement officials were contacted and asked to locate the Kaçmaz family. At 10 a.m. on September 27, 2017, we contacted the media and informed them about the incident. The journalists, who had been following the PakTurk crisis closely from the beginning, were appalled. They said since the family had been abducted in Lahore, they would report the news from there and continuously shared whatever they could learn as development about the incident.

By noon, the news was on the international media. Everyone wanted to know more about the abduction and journalists kept trying to have the latest highlights.

In Lahore, reporters first went to the house where the incident had taken place and then to the nearby police station to collect information. We also requested the journalists to insist the police to issue an FIR about the incident and solicit information from the government agencies to secure the release of the Kaçmaz family from their illegal detention and save them from likely deportation. Later in the day, Pakistani media outlets reported the abduction as the breaking news, while the police was not concerned about the incident and they deliberately issued no incident report.

Students and parents were appalled as they followed the media coverage of the incident. Mobilized, they thought of ways to urge the officials for saving the Kaçmaz family.

When the news spread worldwide, the number of the followers of the @kacmazfamily Twitter account reached 5,000 in a few hours.

On September 27, 2017, at around 4:00 p.m., the wife

of former PakTurk Education Foundation executive board member Murat Ervan, who lived in Islamabad, phoned him and said her car was being followed. While Murat Ervan informed his colleagues, Mrs. Ervan's prudence and calm thwarted the abduction attempt against her and her husband. On the same day the Kaçmaz family's abduction, Mr. and Mrs. Ervan had to move to an undisclosed location and hide.

A colleague later told us that a police squad had raided the residence of his friend Mr. Hıfzı, with whom Mr. Ervan had made a phone call in the day. Having examined the last phone calls he made before changing location, the men in civilian clothes and claiming to be police officers insistently asked the residents to learn Mr. and Mrs. Ervan's whereabouts and threatened to arrest Mr. Hıfzı if he refused to cooperate with the police. They insulted Mr. Hıfzı and showed him a log of Mr. Ervan's last phone calls and said, "He called you the latest; tell us where he is and we will let you be." Mr. Hıfzı tried for minutes to explain to the plain-clothed 'police officers' that he did not know Mr. Murat Ervan's whereabouts. He was eventually saved when the men were fed up and left.

When Mr. Hıfzı called our friends and told them what had happened, our worries increased even more. When a Pakistani colleague advised, "None of your friends should stay in their homes this evening," our friends complied and stayed at their Pakistani colleagues' places. This way, a second abduction wave could be prevented.

During that phase, I had to leave my home. Thinking about whom we might ask to stay for some days, I remembered a journalist friend. I called him and told him about the matter. He said he and his family would be glad to host us. When I said, "But, we need a place for three more families," he was chivalrous and said he could host four families in his house. Hence, our dear friend hosted us for five days. In those days of trouble, our Pakistani friends and colleagues opened their homes to us without expectation. Although they were all aware of the great risk, they still hosted us with no hesitation.

September 28, 2017

Dawn: Former PakTurk Administrator Abducted with Family Human Rights Commission of Pakistan: Kacmaz Family Must Be Released Immediately

Having left their homes, our friends continued staying with the local friends and colleagues. The abduction of the Kaçmaz family headlined on all national channels. The whole country talked about the abduction.

With Mr. Ervan in hiding, the abductors acted. They surveilled our friends with whom Mr. Ervan had a recent phone call. Besides, they exerted physical and psychological pressure on our friends.

Our friends in Lahore kept their cool despite the crisis and repeatedly visited the police station to demand the release of Mr. Mesut Kaçmaz and his family. We later discovered a senior official had called the police station and ordered the officers not to file the incident. Therefore, the abduction of the Kaçmaz family was not officially filed.

Federal government officials, meanwhile, expressed their surprise at the incident, saying a thing like this could not have happened, implying the PakTurk teachers made false statements to the media. They said no state agency had been involved and that the family was not detained by the state authorities.

While it was obvious the abduction had been carried out by the state elements, the authorities passed the ball back and forth in tight spaces. Mr. Fatih Avcu's testimony hinted the abduction had been planned by at least one state agency.

Friends who checked the Turkish Airlines flights departing from Lahore and Islamabad discovered the family could not have been deported from either airport via the Turkish Airlines. They kept vigil and checked at the airports on the second day as well. Consequently, it was believed the family had not been deported and was still detained somewhere in Lahore.

Mr. Mesut Kaçmaz's family and other Turkish teachers were under the UNHCR protection. The abduction of the family meant an international crime. The UNHCR officials were not indifferent to the matter and they demanded an urgent explanation from the Government of Pakistan. Pakistani officials reiterated the same untruth to the UNHCR, stating they did not know where the family was and that they had not been aware of the incident.

The UN offices in Brussels and New York followed the case closely. They asked both Turkiye and Pakistan to take initiatives to resolve the matter and release the family.

The late Asma Jahangir, a world-renowned human rights lawyer who took up the case of the PakTurk teachers, took the matter to the Lahore High Court. She demanded that the

Kaçmaz family be released and not deported. Justice Shams Mahmud Mirza ordered a stay on any possible deportation and ordered the state prosecutor to find the Kaçmaz family and produce them at the court by the next hearing. He then adjourned the hearing until October 6, 2017.

Speaking to the media after the court, Asma Jahangir said she would follow the matter resolutely. "We will exercise all legal means to prevent the government from deporting the Kaçmaz family," she said. Former PakTurk Teacher Fatih Avcu, who witnessed the abduction, also spoke to the media and narrated the incident. He also recorded a video clip about the details of the incident and his experiences and posted it on his Twitter account for the world to see and respond. Under normal circumstances, considering Mr. Fatih Avcu's case, several people might think, "The state released him, why should he get into further trouble again?"; yet, he did not hesitate and took the matter into his own hands. He continued to his activism, even if it was risky, to save his friend and neighbor Mesut Kaçmaz and his family.

We also closely monitored the news on the Turkish media, which acted as the proxy of the incumbent regime in Turkiye in transmuting the abductions of innocent Turkish citizens from various countries into a parade as if it were a great virtue. Daily, we scanned the online papers and news portals to learn if they published anything about the Kaçmaz family.

The Turkish media reported nothing about the deportation. They were obviously glad that the family had been spirited away with sacks over their heads. They were not ashamed to announce such abductions from various countries and especially in Turkiye to the world and the Turkish public opinion with pomp and show through myriad slanders to manage perceptions.

The Human Rights Commission of Pakistan (HRCP) issued a statement calling for the release of the Kaçmaz family. Questions to the Punjab provincial police about this statement, which was reported by Reuters, were not answered.

September 29, 2017

Students and Parents: We Want the Kaçmaz Family Back

It was three days into the abduction of the Kaçmaz family and there was still no news of them. The government officials kept mum other than repeating the incident had nothing to do with the state. Turkish families continued to stay in the homes of their Pakistani friends because of the abduction risk.

Several Pakistani media outlets made live broadcasts in front of the Kaçmaz family's house, demanding government action and the immediate release of the family.

Upset by the incident, students and parents issued a press statement at the Islamabad Press Club and staged a peaceful protest. Calling on the government, the parents demanded an explanation on the whereabouts of the Kaçmaz family. They demanded the family be released. The participants chanted the slogan, "We want the Kaçmaz family back" during the protest.

Meanwhile, the flights to and from Islamabad and Lahore were constantly checked. No development was in sight at the airports about the Kaçmaz family. Turkish media continued to report false news about the family but did not comment on whether they had been deported or not.

September 30, 2017

Campaign on Twitter with the hashtag "#FreedomToKacmazFamily"

While Turkish colleagues continued to stay in groups in the homes of their Pakistani friends and colleagues, the Pakistani media insistently covered the abduction and its aftermath. Television talk shows discussed the incident from various aspects and speculated about the repercussions.

The plain-clothed men who had asked Mr. Murat Ervan's whereabouts were still unknown; yet, they kept pestering those whom he last spoke on the phone and pushed to get proper information about him. The Ervan residence was under 24-hour surveillance. Plain-clothed people also stood guard near Mr. Ervan's car parked by his wife in front of a supermarket close to his house, before making her escape in a passing car.

With two colleagues, I organized a campaign for the release of the Kaçmaz Family on the Twitter account @ kacmazailesi. We tried our best to keep the incident fresh on the Pakistani and the global social media sphere through the hashtag #FreedomToKacmazFamily. Daily campaigns and calls made on social media urged for the immediate release of the family.

Each day added to our hefty concerns about Mr. Mesut Kaçmaz and his family. It was known to many in Pakistan that the abductees might commonly be handed over to radical organizations. Therefore, persistent efforts to rescue the family continued. Despite the official silence, public support grew daily.

September 30, 2017

After the shock of the incident wore off, some Turkish teachers started to return to their homes. For security reasons, two families started sharing the same house.

While the national and international press followed the incident closely, we kept in touch with the daily newspapers and online portals for giving and receiving the latest updates.

Friends could not move fast to leave the country as they thought the airports were not safe and they kept waiting for the appropriate time and conditions.

October 1, 2017

Murat Ervan: Wanted Everywhere!
Pakistan Justice Movement (PTI) Party Spokesperson:
Block Lahore Mall Road and We Will Support You

Mr. Murat Ervan was wanted everywhere. People posing as local law enforcement officials kept harassing and threatening our fellow teachers and administrators. They at times forced their way into the residences of our friends whom they considered vulnerable, using the ways and words similar to the squad who abducted the Kaçmaz family.

The reason the Kaçmaz family had been detained without deportation seemed the abductors' demand to include the Ervan family, who too were insistently wanted by the Turkish authorities, in the bunch. This was evident from the conduct of the squad who kept raiding and harassing residences by unethical and illegal means to locate the Ervan family. The squad assigned for the abduction hid their identities, claiming to be police officers. They probably carried out their top-secret operation with a small group so a few people would know about that. As such, they had planned to abduct the Kaçmaz family in Lahore past midnight and Mr. Murat Ervan and his wife in Islamabad on the next day. This was why they kept detaining the Kaçmaz Family, but the vigilance and composure of Mrs. Ervan spoiled the other part of the plan.

As the squad kept searching for the Ervan Family, they increased the pressure on other Turkish teachers. They even harassed the local cleaners and babysitters who worked in the teachers' homes, asking, "Are there any other Turks staying with the family in the house you work?".

Back then in the opposition, Imran Khan's party PTI kept exerting relentless pressure on the Nawaz Sharif government. In this process, except for one or two feeble voices, the PTI was silent, and no comments were made by the party about the Kaçmaz family. We were to meet the party's spokesperson Fawad Chaudhry and request his support. Chaudhry welcomed me and my friend at his house and we told him about the troubles. We asked him to help us find the Kaçmaz family. We also told him about the troubles of other Turkish families. Chaudhry listened to us and said, "How many of you are there? Block the Mall Road [one of the busiest avenues in Lahore] and we will support you." Taken aback by this suggestion, we said, "We'd rather discuss this with our friends" and left. Until that day, the party had made no statement on the issue. They suggested us to overreact this way.

In Pakistan, whenever they demanded any right, people would block a main artery of the city to have their wish. Society was accustomed to this. The party spokesperson thought he showed us a way out. However, the Turkish teachers, who always believed in the importance of seeking their rights through democratic means and were unwavering in their commitment, found salvation in resorting to legal remedies.

October 2, 2017

Senator Farhatullah Babar: For the first time in the country's history, a foreign family was abducted

Some friends also started exploring alternative ways to leave the country. Due to the risks of leaving from the airports, as an intermediate solution, they started leaving Pakistan by land for safer countries.

The consecutive failures to find Mr. and Mrs. Ervan and the departure of the teachers who could have contacted the family further infuriated the abductors. While we kept on fending ourselves from these people, some Pakistani government officials whose opinions we solicited distorted the incident by saying, "Perhaps the Kaçmaz family has gone on a long trip."

Meanwhile, we contacted the UNHCR officials because Mr. and Mrs. Ervan had disappeared while they were wanted and endangered by abduction and forced deportation. Mr. Murat Ervan was known to the UNHCR Islamabad Office and the officials there. As he was an executive of the PakTurk Education Foundation before being forced to resign by the Government of the Punjab, Mr. Ervan had met with the UNHCR officials before the events escalated. He had received first-hand assurance when he asked, "What are the limits of the UNHCR protection?" and the UNHCR officials replied, "You are under our protection. Pakistan can never deport you to Turkiye."

When we contacted the UNHCR officials in Islamabad to provide Mr. and Mrs. Ervan protection and safe evacuation from Pakistan while the abductors deployed the Pakistani law enforcement against the Turkish teachers, the UNHCR officials did not take the matter seriously and, in contradiction to their promises, failed to protect neither Mr. and Mrs. Ervan nor the other Turkish teachers.

The issue continued to remain a hot topic in public opinion. Senator Farhatullah Babar of the Pakistan People's Party (PPP) submitted a motion in the Senate, demanding answers from the then-Interior Minister Ahsan Iqbal vis-à-vis the Kaçmaz family. He stated that the incident exposed the incompetence of state institutions and resembled other abduction cases that went unpunished in the country's history. Babar also emphasized that, for the first time in Pakistan's history, a foreign family had been abducted.

Seven days into the abduction of the Kaçmaz family, there was still no news. While worries weighed heavier on shoulders daily, the Lahore High Court's decision to halt the family's and the Turkish teachers' likely deportation eased the tension albeit slightly.

October 3, 2017

Lahore High Court: Murat Ervan Cannot be Deported
Islamabad High Court: Turkish Teachers Cannot Be Deported or Subjected to Harassment

The Pakistani media insistently pursued the abduction case and kept the issue on the agenda. Everyone felt sorry for the Kaçmaz family and made efforts for their release.

As the law enforcement searched Mr. Murat Ervan everywhere and the Turkish educator families were constantly harassed, our lawyer took the matter to the Lahore High Court. Justice Shams Mahmud Mirza, the judge hearing the Kaçmaz family's case, ruled that Mr. Ervan cannot be deported. The court ordered the decision be notified to the relevant government departments and security units at airports.

In a case heard in the Islamabad High Court, the Court overruled Turkish teachers' likely deportation and warned the law enforcement not to raid residences.

While we could not reach Mr. Ervan, we were reminded that attempting to leave Pakistan by land was risky. We kept waiting after the high court decisions.

October 4, 2017

Mrs. Meral's student: "We Miss Our Teachers So Much, Give Them Back to Us!"
Zekeriya Özşahin Abducted!

While there was no news of the Kaçmaz family, the state officials continued to maintain their silence. Students and parents of PakTurk Schools Lahore organized a press statement in front of the Lahore Press Club to send a strong message to the government about the abduction of the Kaçmaz family.

Meral Kaçmaz's students participated in the protest, chanting "We want our teachers back". The students told the journalists who interviewed them, "Mrs. Meral is like an angel, she was always concerned about our well-being and education. We miss her so much! We want her back!"

On October 4, 2017, a squad of six plain-clothed men in three cars arrived at the house of a Turkish educator who lived on the same street with Mr. Zekeriya Özşahin, the Turkish principal of a PakTurk educational institution in Islamabad. Having been informed of Mr. Özşahin's presence in that house as a guest, the squad handcuffed him behind his back, blindfolded him, put a sack over his head, and took him to an undisclosed location in front of his family and friends. Mr. Özşahin was released after four hours of torture and detention. Despite severe battery and verbal abuses his abductors inflicted upon him to discourage him from talking about this unlawful act, he stood firm and exercised his legal rights to report this inhumane and unlawful practice to a court and the United Nations High Commissioner for Refugees (UNHCR) office in Islamabad.

October 5, 2017

Students: "Today is Teachers' Day but We Cannot Celebrate"
Mrs. Meral's student Fizza Jumani: "Mrs. Meral was not only my teacher; she was also a mother to me."

On occasion of the October 5 World Teachers' Day, PakTurk

students called for the release of their abducted teachers on social media.

MQM MP Syed Ali Raza Abidi raised the abduction of the Kaçmaz family during a session in the National Assembly of Pakistan. "A foreign couple under the United Nations protection was abducted from their home with their daughters! The state is silent! Mr. President, are we a banana republic or a constitutional state?" he questioned, criticizing the government.

Islamabad PakTurk students staged their second protest in front of the Islamabad Press Club on the Teachers' Day. They demanded the recovery of the Kaçmaz family.

Foreign Minister Khawaja M. Asif could not give clear answers to Turkish journalist Sıtkı Özcan, who directed him questions about the abducted Kaçmaz family during a talk organized at a Washington D.C. think tank. He blatantly lied, claiming that the Turkish teachers' UNHCR asylum seeker documents had expired on September 30, 2017, and that the Pakistani government had no responsibility for the human tragedy in the wake of the expulsion decision and the abduction of the Kaçmaz family.

Meanwhile, the UNHCR certificates of the Turkish staff of the PakTurk Schools would expire on November 28, 2017. It was inconceivable that the Pakistani Foreign Minister had not known this, even though the UNHCR protection given to the Turkish teachers was widely reported in the media and was well known even to the general public. Khawaja M. Asif went down in the annals of his country's history with his blatant lie.

Students congratulated Mesut and Meral Kaçmaz on the Teachers' Day via social media. They shared the letters they wrote to their teachers. In one letter, Mrs. Meral's student Fizza Jumani wrote: "Mrs. Meral was my teacher and the best three years of my life had been spent in her class. She was not only my teacher but also a mother to me. She would help and guide me the same she would her own child. I have never seen such a beautiful family." She defended her teacher and wrote #FreedomfortheKacmazFamily on her placard.

October 6, 2017
Senator Muhammad Mohsin Khan Leghari: Turkish Teachers Provide Quality Education to Our Children, They Have Done a Great Service to Our Country.

Ten days after the abduction of the Kaçmaz family, there was still no news of them. Without losing an iota of hope, our colleagues kept struggling round the clock for the recovery and release of the family. They were in constant contact with the government officials besides media outlets.

On September 28, the case in the Lahore High Court was adjourned until October 6, 2017. Our lawyer, the late Asma Jahangir, and colleagues at the court had eagerly waited to hear what the state prosecutor would say. In the previous hearing, the judge had ordered the prosecutor to find out where the Kaçmaz family was. The hearing started and the judge gave the state prosecutor the floor. The prosecutor said, "I conducted a probe on the Kaçmaz family and have ascertained that the family is not in state custody by any means." Hearing this, Judge Mirza became furious and said, "I give you time until October 16, find this family!" He also said to the local authorities about the teachers who keep having security problems, "Ensure the safety of these people!" and ruled that the teachers would not be deported. He summoned the station-house officer of the police station who had not registered the FIR (First Incident Report) after the abduction of the Kaçmaz family and directly ordered him to file a report on the case.

Speaking to a crowd of reporters after the trial, Asma Jahangir said, "Are we a country governed by the law of the jungle? Since when do we abduct people and hand them over to the dictators of the world? I know the perpetrators of this incident and I will not let them go easy!"

Senator Muhammad Mohsin Khan Leghari said, "Turkish teachers provide quality education to our children and they have done a great service to our country. The case of the Kaçmaz family must be solved and we must not be involved with Turkiye's internal affairs."

The campaign titled "Free the Kaçmaz Family and Do Not Disturb Turkish Teachers" on change.org amassed 1000 signatures in a short time. The signatures were forwarded with a petition to the erstwhile Pakistani Prime Minister Shahid Khaqan Abbasi.

October 7, 2017
Karachi PakTurk Students: Justice Delayed is Justice Denied, Release the Kaçmaz Family!

Street interviews were conducted in many cities about the abduction of the Kaçmaz family. People expressed their sorrow over the incidents and said the family should be released immediately.

In Karachi, PakTurk students organized a protest in front of the Karachi Press Club. They wore a mask of Mesut Kaçmaz's face and protested with the following statement: "We want justice for the Kaçmaz family, justice delayed is not justice, we demand his immediate release!"

The Pakistani staff of the PakTurk Schools in Quetta organized a Day of Solidarity and Prayer to support the Turkish teachers, to which parents were also invited.

Students across Pakistan shared personal statement videos on social media in reaction to the abduction of the Kaçmaz family.

October 8, 2017
Pakistani MP Syed Ali Raza Abidi:
Kaçmaz family abducted two weeks ago,
whereabouts unknown.

Twelve days after the abduction of the Kaçmaz family, there was still no news of their fate. The state did not claim responsibility, while no information could be accessed on the whereabouts of the family. Colleagues scanned the news reports in the Turkish media daily, and monitored the Turkish Airlines flights at major airports to check if there were any developments.

The abduction incident, a hot topic in the country, kept getting attention across Pakistan and everyone wanted the family to be found. PakTurk alumni in Quetta held a press conference and reiterated their call for the immediate release of the Kaçmaz family. "Justice must be done for the Kaçmaz family and they, who have done no harm to the country, must be allowed to return home," they stated.

Mesut Kaçmaz's parents took to social media and called on the Pakistani government to find their son and release him immediately.

MQM MP Syed Ali Raza Abidi tweeted, "It's been two weeks since the Kaçmaz family was abducted and their whereabouts are unknown."

October 9, 2017

PakTurk alumni in Lahore issued a statement, this time at the Lahore Press Club, and reiterated their demands to elucidate the incident and secure the immediate release of the Kaçmaz family.

Local media paid close attention to the press conferences. They interviewed participants and the public and covered the programs. While everyone kept wondering where the Kaçmaz family was, the government's indifference continued unabated.

October 10, 2017

Reactions to the abduction of the Kaçmaz family continued. PakTurk Karachi graduates convened at the school and protested against the abduction.

In those days, Mesut Kaçmaz's friend Mr. Mehmet wrote a letter to Mr. Mesut including these lines of poetry:

Teacher Mesut, who were you?

You left all Pakistanis wondering.

They took you away from your home on a dark night!

How some big boys were scared of a teacher!

October 11, 2017
Washington Post: A Turkish Family Goes Missing,
Eyes on Intelligence Agencies

Not only in Pakistan but all over the world, the media kept the abduction in Pakistan on their agenda. Everyone demanded the Pakistani authorities to find the family.

A social media user took a picture with a placard that read "Freedom for Kaçmaz Family" and shared it on social media, which soon turned into a huge campaign and the picture was shared thousands of times.

A group of Turkish nationals in Canada announced they would stage a protest in front of the Pakistani Embassy in Toronto on October 13 to push the recovery of the Kaçmaz family.

In Lahore, parents issued another press statement and asked the government, "Where is the Kaçmaz family?" calling for their immediate release.

The Washington Post published a significant news article about the abduction of the Kaçmaz family. For the first time, a major international newspaper shared the claim that the abduction might have been carried out by the Pakistani intelligence. "A Turkish family has disappeared and the eyes are on intelligence agencies," the Washington Post headlined its report.

October 12, 2017

Kerim Balci: On September 27, we will remind the whole world of this crime against humanity

MQM MP Syed Ali Raza Abidi released a video calling on national and international organizations to locate and recover the Kaçmaz family.

In a video statement, journalist Kerim Balcı addressed the Pakistani authorities, "Release the abducted Kaçmaz Family. We will not forget and forgive this crime against humanity. We will remind the whole world of this crime against humanity on every September 27, the day the Kaçmaz family was abducted."

Journalist and author Emine Eroğlu, posted on her social media account, "A Pakistani friend could not look me in the eye. Her eyes were full as she said, "Is there no end to our embarrassment towards you?"

October 13, 2017

A Public Protest in Toronto

Seventeen days after the abduction of the Kaçmaz family, there was still no news about their condition and whereabouts. Concerns kept growing, but the local and international support boosted our morale. Our hope for the Kaçmaz Family would be released soon remained strong.

October 13, 2017 marked the first international protest after the abduction of the Kaçmaz family. A group of Turkish and Canadian nationals with common sense gathered in front of the Pakistani Embassy in Toronto and made a press statement. This protest against the Pakistani government was also broadcasted live on social media and became a hot topic in Pakistan.

October 14, 2017

"Rule of Law Failed in Pakistan, Kaçmaz Family Deported"

Eighteen days into the abduction of the Kaçmaz family, the Pakistani government kept withholding information about their condition and whereabouts. Colleagues in Karachi continued working for elucidating the case and their search for the Kaçmaz family. This time, a larger group protested in front of the UNHCR office in Karachi against UNHCR's slow action to find the Kaçmaz family and urged the agency to be more active in locating and having the family released.

Simultaneously, school officials and students in Peshawar held a rally calling on the government to find the family and demanded their release.

While each development on the issue was assessed, a news report in the Turkish media changed the agenda. The news reported that the Kaçmaz family had been 'extradited' to Turkiye. The news report, without photos or videos, reported how the Kaçmaz family had been flown to Turkiye.

The release of the couple's daughters and our colleagues' subsequent contact with them confirmed the news.

The pro-Erdogan media, which published false news until the family was illegally deported to Turkiye, wrote in detail how the Kaçmaz family had been abducted, who abducted them, and which organization in Pakistan carried out the operation. The Pakistani government authorities never owned the incident, they kept denying it, feigning ignorance every time. Once the regime in Turkiye got what it wanted, it broke its promise to Pakistan which was, "We will give you what you want, but it will not be reported in the media. It will remain a secret that the abduction had been jointly carried out by our states." The Turkish media revealed most details through political pomp and show and praised the international crime committed by the Pakistani state in tandem with Turkiye.

<u>October 15, 2017</u>

Lawyer Asma Jahangir: We Will Have All Aspects of the Incident Elucidated

National and international media covered the incident as breaking news. All over the world, the incident was described as a crime against humanity. On social media, people took it further and criticized Pakistan severely.

It is noteworthy that the deportation of the Kaçmaz family took place only two days before the hearing at the Lahore High Court. The court demanded to see the family at the hearing on October 16, 2017, and it was understood the deportation had been carried out in a hurry because while the Government of Pakistan could say nothing, the game was revealed through the exciting reports filed by the Turkish media, covering everything in detail.

The judge of the Lahore High Court was shown the news reports from the Turkish media. The reports explained that the Kaçmaz family had been deported through a private jet to Turkiye. Trying to make sense of what he had heard and seen, the judge turned to the chief prosecutor of the state and asked for an explanation. Angered by the prosecutor's indifferent stance and lack of interest, the judge ordered an urgent written explanation and clarification.

Lawyer Asma Jahangir made harsh statements to the media after the hearing and said, "If the Foreign Minister and the Interior Minister do not know what happened, then there is a third person and I know it, we will get to the root of this incident." The family had their passports at home when they were abducted. Showing the passports to journalists, Jahangir said the Turkish educators could not have left Pakistan without their passports and that since they had been extradited, this could not have happened without the permission of a higher authority.

While everyone strongly condemned the illegal deportation of the Kaçmaz Family to Turkiye, people worldwide who followed the case sensitively started calling us to protest against Pakistan for this decision in various cities abroad. The protests for the release of the Kaçmaz family turned into protests condemning Pakistan after the forced 'extradition' and people convened in world capitals to condemn Pakistan.

October 16, 2017
Lahore High Court:
Government Must Make Official Statement

The forced deportation of the Kaçmaz family to Turkiye headlined on all national channels and newspapers. The Lahore High Court ordered the respective institutions to provide us an official letter explaining how the incident had happened. The government, which paid little attention to the court before the extradition decision, sent no letter to the court.

October 17, 2017
Dawn: This Disgraceful Government Decision Against
Turkish Citizens in Pakistan Must Be the Last and Must
Not Be Allowed to Happen Again

Pakistan's prestigious English newspaper Dawn, which followed the incident from its inception, analyzed the issue in its editorial and emphasized these points:

We learned that, because of a startling executive power, a Turkish family protected by the UNHCR had been returned to Turkiye despite a high court ruling in Pakistan.

Notwithstanding the tenets of domestic and international laws, the abduction of the Turkish family in Lahore was cruel and the Pakistani authorities' decision to extradite the family is nothing short of state insensitivity. Undoubtedly, whatever the imperatives of maintaining close relations with the regime of Turkish President Erdogan, Pakistan needs not violate her own laws and international obligations to placate a foreign country

Indeed, when it comes to Pakistan's legitimate objections to the malicious actions of other states, the case of the Kaçmaz family weakens Pakistan's case.

The United States, for example, made tough demands on Pakistan in the past and even countries with which Pakistan has difficult relations, such as India, can and do use Turkiye's fulfillment of unreasonable demands to get Pakistan to have their demands met. Surely, a way other than a secret extradition operation should have been possible in the Turkish family's case.

A major concern is the flagrant violation of the High Court decisions. High Courts rightly establish a system of checks and balances among the institutions in the country. Perhaps the authorities responsible for the forced extradition have an official and legally defensible reason, but this explanation should be requested by the judiciary and made public.

Ultimately, if the right to legal protection of any resident of Pakistan is not ensured, everyone in the country, citizen and non-citizen alike, is affected. Missing persons has been a bitter reality in the law for more than a decade.

While all institutions always emphasize the rule of law, very few seem willing to act under the reality and the spirit of the rule of law. This disgraceful decision by the state regarding Turkish citizens in Pakistan should be the last and should neither be allowed nor accepted to be repeated again.

October 18, 2017
Human Rights Watch: Turkish Teachers Left Behind Also at Risk

After the extradition, the Lahore High Court, which followed the case, dispatched its decision to the state institutions for protecting the remaining Turkish educators and preventing the same incident from happening again, and ordered the government to make an immediate statement on the forced extradition of the Kaçmaz family. The Court also ordered the Directorate General of Civil Aviation Authority to submit to the Court all flight manifests in Pakistan on October 14 and 15. It was later confirmed that no record of the Kaçmaz family had been found in the records submitted to the Court. This confirmed the Turkish media reports that the Kaçmaz family had been spirited away from Pakistan on a private jet without any registration.

Renowned Pakistani journalist Shahzeb Khanzada hosted then-Punjab Law Minister Rana Sanaullah on his talk show and asked him about the Kaçmaz family. Rana Sanaullah was the same Minister who had promised to resolve the Turkish educators' pending visa extensions through appointing trustees to the management of the PakTurk Education Foundation, but none of his promises had materialized. Exercising the usual governmental nonchalance and lies since the beginning of the crisis, Minister Sanaullah told Khanzada he had not been aware of either the Kaçmaz family or their extradition. He ignored the twenty-day non-stop reports in the national and international media.

Human Rights Watch (HRW) issued a statement highlighting that the forced deportation of the Kaçmaz family endangered the remaining families who could face the same fate.

October 19, 2017

Member of the European Parliament, Rebecca Harms: How Can This Happen Despite the High Court's Decision and UNHCR Protection?

The first protest in front of the Pakistani Embassy in London condemned the Pakistani government for the forced deportation of the Kaçmaz family. The protesters condemned Pakistan in their press statement. They also called on the Turkish government to "release the Kaçmaz family" and ensure that the incident would not repeat against the remaining teachers in Pakistan.

The second protest was held in front of the Pakistani Embassy in Vienna. The protesters called on the Turkish government to "release the Kaçmaz family" and carried placards reading "We condemn Pakistan! They were just teachers!" and "Vienna is with you!"

Rebecca Harms, a member of the European Parliament, reacted to the forced deportation, in a message, "How is this possible despite the ruling of the Supreme Court and the UNHCR protection? The United Nations must provide an explanation," while criticizing the Pakistani government for the decision.

October 21, 2017

Turkish Teachers' Protest

Turkish teachers in Pakistan protested against the forced deportation. "We are law-abiding people!", "Do not play with our future!" and "Raise your voice for the Turkish teachers!", the teachers chanted in Karachi.

On the same day, Turkish teachers in Quetta issued a statement at the Quetta Press Club, condemning the Government of Pakistan for its decision and called for an end to the pressure and repression.

Kenneth Roth, former head of Human Rights Watch, included the tragedy of the Kaçmaz family alongside the genocide in Burma and the bombing of civilians in Somalia in his Twitter post on the week's most prominent human rights crises.

October 22, 2017

Vienna-based "1 Stimme – 1 Schritt" (One Voice One Step) Association issued a press release condemning the Pakistani government and calling on Turkiye to release the Kaçmaz family.

October 23, 2017

The Asian Human Rights Commission has launched an appeal campaign against the forced extradition of the Kaçmaz family, stating that the Pakistani government violated the court's ruling and the UNHCR's asylum-seeker status requirements, and launched a letter campaign on their website to send to the Pakistani authorities.

October 26, 2017

The Human Rights Commission of Pakistan (HRCP), in a joint statement with the International Federation for Human Rights (FIDH), said the 285 Turkish teachers and their families were at risk of forced deportation.

<u>October 27, 2017</u>

The statements issued by the FIDH and HRCP were reported by the local and international news agencies as breaking news. Several print and broadcast media outlets in Pakistan shared the news with their subscribers and the public.

<u>October 28, 2017</u>

Senate Chairman Raza Rabbani: Interior Ministry Should Issue Written Statement

After PPP Senator Farhatullah Babar submitted a motion on the forced deportation of the Kaçmaz family in the Senate of Pakistan and shared his findings, Senate Chairman Raza Rabbani decreed the Ministry of Interior should make an official statement to the Senate on this issue.

Sharing his findings on the incident in the Senate, Senator Babar stated that the Turkish President Erdogan and the Republic of Turkiye are friends of Pakistan. However, he warned against importing Turkiye's domestic issues into Pakistan.

Senator Babar's statement was picked up by the media and widely-read newspapers across the country.

The abduction and forced deportation of the Kaçmaz family remained on the country's agenda for a month uninterrupted and grew into a most-talked-about issue in the country. While everyone said the Turkish teachers in Pakistan were treated unfairly, that the schools they had built with their own hard work had been usurped from them unfairly, and that it was wrong for Pakistan to fetch Turkiye's internal affairs into the country, the government of Nawaz Sharif preferred to remain silent and played possum in response to the public outcry and the questions posed by the media.

Following the forced deportation of the Kaçmaz family to Turkiye, the actions for securing their immediate release continued uninterrupted. Significant initiatives were taken with the involvement of the United Nations. Since the family had been unde the UNHCR protection, Pakistan's forced deportation of the family had also been against the international law. The United Nations had been ineffective due to the Pakistani government's effective concealment of the events and lack of explanation; however, after the family's forced deportation to Turkiye, the issue became clearer and we could witness a more active United Nations working for the family's release.

After the forced deportation of the Kaçmaz family to Turkiye, we contacted the couple's daughters, who were released on arrival to Turkiye, and asked what they had experienced. The daughters' accounts were recorded and played to the judge who heard the case in the Lahore High Court on September 15. The transcript of the conversation was also submitted as the strongest evidence of the forced deportation of the family to Turkiye.

The children were still reeling from the shock of their dastardly experience. They described the events in detail. They said, on the night of September 27, 2017, about 15 armed men and women in plainclothes and uniforms raided their house, bundled their parents and themselves into separate cars, draped sacks over their heads, and beat their parents. They said the windows of their detention place were sealed and painted and they were not allowed to go outside. They said their guards told them they would not be extradited to Turkiye and that they were detained supposedly for their own protection.

The officials told them they wished to make the family meet the Turkish Ambassador before their 'extradition'. The girls said they were put in a car while blindfolded and they were told they would be taken to Islamabad. When they removed the blindfolds, they saw they were at an airfield and a jet was waiting for them. They said they resisted against getting on the plane but were forced on board, handcuffed, and insulted during the entire flight. They said their father was arrested and transferred to Istanbul, and their mother was taken to Ankara.

We retained a lawyer for the defense of the Kaçmaz family in Turkiye. During the process, Mrs. Meral Kaçmaz was released after six months in solitary confinement. Mr. Mesut Kaçmaz was incarcerated in Silivri Prison.

Meanwhile, the entire process was constantly followed up with the United Nations offices and authorities. On May 25, 2018, the result of our colleagues' appeal for the release of the Kaçmaz family to the UN Human Rights Council (OHCHR), where cases of arbitrary detention are heard, was announced. The United Nations ruled for the immediate and unconditional release of the unlawfully and forcibly abducted Kaçmaz family, for Turkiye and Pakistan to pay compensation for material and moral damages, and for the punishment of the officials involved in the abduction. With this ruling, our hope for the release of Mr. Mesut Kaçmaz increased. During his hearing on July 4, 2018, the United Nations ruling was presented to the court and Mr. Mesut Kaçmaz was released.

After their release, Mr. Mesut Kaçmaz and his wife Mrs. Meral Kaçmaz spoke about the victimization they had suffered in Pakistan and Turkiye and described the physical and psychological torture they had gone through. The couple said, although they had been abducted past midnight in Lahore, Pakistan, with sacks over their heads and blindfolds over their eyes, they were convinced the place they were detained for 18 days was a military compound in the Lahore Cantonment, known as the military headquarters and a posh residential area of Lahore. They could conclude so based on their knowledge of the city and inferring from the titles and the addresses of the businesses on the packages of consumables the abductors occasionally brought to the family. They could also sense the military nature of their location by the voices of people visiting the compound. Although the Pakistani government and the media outlets carefully avoided providing details about the abduction of the Kaçmaz family, the statement "Pakistan's Counter-Terrorism Department abducted the family and handed them over to the Turkish Intelligence" in the pro-Erdogan media in Turkiye provided sufficient preliminary information. However, we might soon learn about the oft-rumored role of Pakistan's Inter-Services Intelligence in the abduction.

Students hold signs as they chant slogans during a protest on the premises of PAKTURK International Schools & Colleges in Karachi, Pakistan November 25, 2016. © 2016 Akhtar Soomro/Reuters

On Sunday, the Pakistani government deported a Turkish educator and his family living in Pakistan back to Turkey, despite their being registered as asylum seekers by the United Nations High Commissioner for Refugees (UNHCR), according to media reports.

Mesut Kaçmaz, his wife and two daughters were picked up from their Lahore home on September 27, allegedly by law enforcement officers. Kaçmaz, a well-known educator, was the former vice president of the PakTurk International Schools and Colleges in Pakistan. The family's UNHCR asylum seeker certificate was valid until November 24, 2017.

fidh
INTERNATIONAL FEDERATION
FOR HUMAN RIGHTS
TAKE ACTION
285 Turkish teachers and families risk forcible deportation and persecution
PRESS RELEASE
SAFEGAURD
MY
TEACHERS
MY COUNTRY WILL STAND

The Washington Post
Democracy Dies in Darkness

ASIA & PACIFIC

A Turkish family has disappeared in Pakistan, and suspicion turns to intelligence agencies

By Haq Nawaz Khan and Pamela Constable
October 11, 2017 at 4:35 p.m. EDT

Pakistani students at a PakTurk international school comfort a Turkish teacher facing deportation in Lahore in late 2016. (K.M. Chaudary/AP)

Share   Comment 0

PESHAWAR, Pakistan — A commotion in the downstairs unit of a house shared by schoolteachers from Turkey woke the neighbors. A Turkish school official and his family were being taken away in the night.

Mesut Kacmaz, his wife and two daughters were restrained, blindfolded and hustled into unmarked pickup trucks in Lahore last month by more than a dozen plainclothes security agents, according to Fatih Avci, a neighbor and fellow teacher. When he tried to intervene, Avci said, he was also handcuffed and hooded, and transported to a secret facility.

Are you on Telegram? Subscribe to our channel for the latest updates on Russia's war in Ukraine. →

"The police officers were pushing and shoving to arrest them," Avci said

REUTERS

MIDDLE EAST & NORTH AFRICA   OCTOBER 16, 2017 / 6:08 AM / 3 YEARS AGO

Pakistan deports Turkish school network's former director and family

Saad Sayeed   3 MIN READ

ISLAMABAD (Reuters) - Pakistan has deported a former director of a chain of private Turkish schools along with his family, former school officials said on Monday, the day set for a court hearing on the deportation.

Asma Jilani Jahangir, renowned Pakistani human rights lawyer and social activist who co-founded and chaired the Human Rights Commission of Pakistan and the lawyer of the members of the Kaçmaz family who were abducted and deported illegally to Turkey, is adamant to clamp down the abduction and illegal deportation scandal.

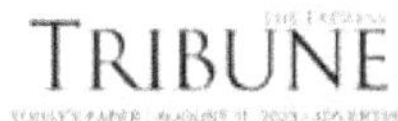

No record available: Mystery shrouds Turkish family's 'deportation'

FIA sources say IBMS record only shows Mesut Kacmaz's arrival at Lahore in June 2016

Qadeer Tanoli   October 18, 2017

Mesut Kacmaz, a former principal of the Pak-Turk School, his wife and two teenage daughters were whisked away from their WAPDA Town house on September 27. PHOTO: FILE

ISLAMABAD: Deep mystery surrounds the reported deportation of Mesut Kacmaz, an official of the Pak-Turk School, and his family as no record of the extradition is available with the concerned authorities in Pakistan.

According to media reports, the Turk official and his family were flown out on a jet of the Turkish Airlines from Islamabad on Oct 14.

"There were Turkish police officers on the plane and the victims were handed over to them," a report claimed. It added the Turkish authorities had taken the couple into their custody while the children were living with their grandparents.

However, the concerned quarters are still silent about their deportation from Pakistan and it remains a secret whether they were actually deported or not.

Revealed: 'Missing' former PakTurk School principal, family deported on Oct 14

Sources in the Interior Ministry and the Federal Investigation Agency (FIA) told *The Express Tribune* that there is no record of any such deportation at Integrated Border Management System (IBMS), a system installed at the airports to check computerised arrival and departure of any traveler.

The sources said the IBMS record only shows arrival of Kacmaz – having passport number U03690406 – on June 6, 2016 via flight EY 241 at Lahore Airport, but there is no record of his departure.

DAWN

Footprints: THE DARK SIDE

Published October 8, 2017

STAFF members of Pak-Turk School's campus in Karachi on Saturday stage a protest demonstration outside the Karachi Press Club for the recovery of the Kacmaz family, who were recently picked up in Lahore and taken away to an unknown location — Fahim Siddiqi / White Star

THEY travel in groups now, never alone; and each time the doorbell rings, they dread the worst. Their homes are becoming emptier; personal possessions are being sold off.

The Turkish community here is scared. Teachers by profession, they live in identity-less limbo, squashed between two countries. They have neither visas for living in Pakistan, nor — for fear of being arrested — can they return to Turkey. After their last visas expired, they did not receive an extension; they were given a stay for a year by the Lahore High Court, and they have UNHCR asylum-seeker certificates.

The fear and insecurity have deepened after the Kacmaz family was recently picked up and taken away to an unknown location. When Fatih Avcu heard a commotion in the home of the ex-principal of the Pak-Turk School, Mesut Kacmaz, he rushed downstairs to see what was happening but was mistakenly picked up too.

"They carried huge guns, but were in civvies, so we don't know who they were," says Avcu. "They put black hoods on all of us, even Kacmaz's wife and teenaged daughters, handcuffed us and drove for around 30 minutes before stopping somewhere. It was a fully furnished house, but I don't know where we were." Later, Avcu was told he wasn't supposed to be there and was dropped blindfolded near his house. "I walked home from the crossing," he says.

The Washington Post

Pakistan is set to expel more than 100 schoolteachers at Turkey's request

By Max Bearak

November 17, 2016 at 11:39 a.m. EST

Hussain, Khalid. Pak-Turk Schhol System.
The Nation, Nov 20, 2016

HOME LATEST PAKISTAN BUSINESS WORLD OPINION SCI-TECH LIFE & STYLE T-MAGAZINE T.EDIT SPORTS BLOGS VIDEOS SLIDE

PakTurk school staff challenges expulsion orders

Say petitioners, their families were 'condemned unheard'

Rizwan Shehzad   November 16, 2016

Say petitioners, their families were 'condemned unheard'. PHOTO: REUTERS

ISLAMABAD: Officials of the PakTurk Educational Foundation challenged on Wednesday the interior ministry's orders in the Islamabad High Court.

Pak Turk Schools employees in UN protection after visa extensions turned down

Inamullah Khattak | Published February 11, 2017

As many as 108 Turkish employees of the Pak Turk Schools, along with their families, have been in the United Nations' (UN) protection after Pakistani authorities denied them an extension in their visas to work in the country, DawnNews reported.

Documents available with DawnNews reveal that the individuals had requested the UN's refugee agency, UNHCR, that they be resettled in a country other than Turkey after Pakistan ordered to deport them.

The applicants had told UNHCR they feared arrest, coercion and torture by the Erdogan government in Turkey in case the Pakistani government forcibly deported them to Istanbul.

Chapter 6

Transfer of the PakTurk Schools
to the Turkiye Maarif Foundation

(September 15, 2017 –
December 13, 2018)

The Turkish Embassy in Islamabad remained silent after the abduction of the Kaçmaz family and avoided making any statement. It probably waited for the arrest and extradition of the remaining Turkish educators to Turkiye.

The Embassy kept working round the clock to materialize the transfer of the PakTurk Schools and exerted constant pressure on the Government of Pakistan. The way the handover had not taken place in the wake of psychological damage and pressure on the Turkish educators caused dissatisfaction in Ankara and the Turkish Ambassador in Islamabad was blamed for having failed. Ankara, and Erdogan in particular, was consumed with ambition and kept embarking on extraordinary efforts to have the PakTurk Schools transferred to the Turkiye Maarif Foundation (TMF).

When the handover of the Schools did not happen as quickly as expected, Ankara blamed the Ambassador and replaced him with a new one loyal to Erdogan and whom they believed could solve the problem. Sadık Babür Girgin was officially replaced by İhsan Mustafa Yurdakul as the Ambassador of the Republic of Turkiye in Islamabad on December 29, 2017. However, the former Ambassador Girgin had traveled to Turkiye on October 14, 2017 on the same private aircraft with the abducted Kaçmaz family on board and had overseen this international crime against humanity. When the tide turned, Sadık Babür Girgin, likely to be punished under the UN OHCR decision demanding the punishment of all officials involved in the abduction of the Kaçmaz family, was replaced by İhsan Mustafa Yurdakul, whose first task was to ensure the handover of the PakTurk Schools.

The Pakistani government, not wishing to boost the public outcry over the abduction of the Kaçmaz family and their subsequent unwarranted extradition to Turkiye, had delayed the PakTurk Schools issue with the same tactics and "Let us wait and see" policy it had implemented in the visa extension crisis. Meanwhile, official visits between Turkiye and Pakistan continued frequently and negotiations on the PakTurk Schools continued. Pakistan kept stalling Turkiye on transferring the schools and making Turkiye wait until it got what it wanted. Erdogan visited Pakistan twice, the Pakistani Prime Minister traveled to Turkiye, and dozens of high-level bilateral visits took place. Yet, the transfer of the schools was not achieved. This angered Erdogan, who reacted against Pakistan, which he considered a second-class country. Erdogan would each time indicate the transfer of the PakTurk Schools as a pre-condition to sign the free trade agreement between Turkiye and Pakistan.

PakTurk Schools continued its education uninterrupted, making every effort to ensure the students were not adversely affected. With the decisions of the Islamabad High Court, the inspections carried out to pressure the schools had ceased and a partial relief prevailed. During the inspections, the officials made unreasonable demands on the school administration. They demanded that lightning rods, which are not even present in several government buildings in Pakistan, be installed in the school buildings. Despite everything, the schools fulfilled the demands.

POLITICAL TENSIONS IN PAKISTAN: HARD DAYS AHEAD FOR THE PAKTURK SCHOOLS

To better understand the crisis the PakTurk Schools went through and the circumstances we had to brace as the Turkish educators in Pakistan, it would help to take a brief look at the political history of Pakistan and the political battles in Islamabad, the capital of Pakistan. When the Nawaz Sharif government came to power in 2013, it promised to rapidly implement projects and initiatives that would develop the country in various fields, especially in the economy. Nawaz Sharif's brother Shehbaz Sharif had been the Chief Minister of the Punjab province, the largest in Pakistan, since 2008. Nawaz Sharif government announced huge projects such as airports, bridges, roads, hospitals, and metrobus networks across Pakistan under the China-Pakistan Economic Corridor (CPEC) agreement. The largest project in the country's history and worth 56 billion dollars, CPEC was signed during Nawaz Sharif's term.

A zero-problem policy was adopted with the neighboring countries. Peace negotiations with India were in progress with preliminary talks with the Indian Prime Minister. Within this frame, the Indian PM visited Islamabad even for a short time to attend Nawaz Sharif's birthday party. The event was met with surprise in both countries. Nawaz Sharif's stance was monitored with concern by the Pakistani military, which was uncomfortable with rapprochements.

Nawaz Sharif served as the Chief Minister of Punjab, Pakistan's largest province (with a population of over 100 million), between 1985 and 1990, and as Prime Minister of

Pakistan between 1990 and 1993, 1997 and 1999 and 2013 and 2017. When he first came to power, Nawaz Sharif pursued a conservative policy in continuation of the Zia-ul-Haq era and continued the Islamization policies. Several private businesses and organizations nationalized during the Zia-ul-Haq era were privatized. Nawaz Sharif, who steered politics with new policies to revitalize the private sector, was implicated in the cooperatives corruption in 1992. He fell out with the President in 1993 after it was found he had been involved in deep corruption. He was forced to resign before the end of his term, triggering a crisis when the President joined forces with the erstwhile Chief of General Staff and dissolved the parliament.

Nawaz Sharif, who reverted to office in 1997, started by taking controversial decisions and steps disturbing the dominant elements in the country. After the constitutional crisis he caused in 1997, his unconventional appointment of General Pervez Musharraf, who was deemed inexperienced to become the Chief of the Army, and the heavy criticism of the force commanders, especially the Air Force Chief, for Musharraf's inability to manage the aftermath of the Indian attack on a Pakistani frigate, General Pervez Musharraf staged a coup in October 1999 and overthrew the Nawaz Sharif government, exiling him and his family to Saudi Arabia. In his book, 'In the Line of Fire', General Musharraf wrote, "If King Fahd of Saudi Arabia had not intervened, Nawaz Sharif would have been executed."

Nawaz Sharif arrived in Lahore five days after Benazir Bhutto's return from exile in 2007, when the cases against her had been dismissed by the Supreme Court of Pakistan. As the late Turkish PM and President Süleyman Demirel used to say, "I was deposed six times and came back seven times," Nawaz Sharif was welcomed by huge crowds. This political change was disturbing General Musharraf. He had gone to Saudi Arabia to persuade with the King to prevent Nawaz from returning to Pakistan. The Saudi King had refused, saying to Musharraf, "You allowed Benazir, why not Nawaz?" because he did favor Nawaz Sharif to lead Pakistan. Musharraf had returned empty-handed.

Pakistan prepared for the general elections while the political tensions kept rising. Benazir Bhutto was assassinated in Rawalpindi in December 2007. This assassination abruptly upset the politics and the agenda across the country. Although radical organizations claimed responsibility for Benazir Bhutto's death, the real perpetrators are still unknown. The incident accelerated the departure of General Pervez Musharraf from Pakistan. Benazir Bhutto's Pakistan People's Party (PPP), won the elections in 2008. Nawaz Sharif's Pakistan Muslim League-Nawaz (PML-N) entered the National Assembly as the main opposition.

Rising to power in the 2013 elections, Nawaz Sharif had General Musharraf arrested and imprisoned to settle a score from the past. The powerful general of the past, who went into exile through the intervention of the military, would suffer the same fate as Nawaz Sharif. While Nawaz Sharif had pursued a conservative policy when he first came to power, he adopted a more liberal policy when he became the Prime Minister in 2013. The Nawaz government had always conflicted with the Pakistan Army and the power elite. He had several frictions with the newly appointed Chief of the Army

Staff, General Qamar Javed Bajwa, and became a persona non grata with the army. When the Panama Papers were leaked to the press in 2016, quoting Nawaz Sharif, his daughter Maryam Safdar, sons and son-in-law, the opposition had an opportunity, and the Pakistan Tehrik-e Insaaf (PTI) leader Imran Khan filed a case at the Supreme Court of Pakistan for the disqualification and arrest of Nawaz Sharif and his associates. The trial between April 15, 2016 and July 28, 2017 concluded with the disqualification of Nawaz Sharif. The court also ruled to investigate further corruption claims in an open case at an accountability court. After Nawaz Sharif's disqualification, his party's Shahid Khaqan Abbasi took office as the interim prime minister.

At the time of the PakTurk Schools crisis, the country's political environment was volatile and the ruling party faced serious problems. On November 16, 2016, a few months before the deportation order against the Turkish teachers of the PakTurk Schools, corruption charges were filed against the government and the PTI-led opposition staged protests in capital Islamabad. Demonstrators demanded Nawaz Sharif's resignation. Before the abduction of the Kaçmaz family on September 27, 2017, Nawaz Sharif was dismissed on July 28, 2017 and Shahid Khaqan Abbasi was appointed as the interim prime minister. Nawaz Sharif, who could not make peace with the army, lost power before the end of his normal term, this time through an army-influenced decision.

IMRAN KHAN'S RISE TO POWER: DARK CLOUDS CROWD OVER THE PAKTURK SCHOOLS

The government was under pressure on multiple fronts across the country. It was an open secret that the Pakistan Army did not want to work with Nawaz Sharif as the Prime Minister. The visa extensions and residence permits of the Turkish teachers were revoked, the Kaçmaz family was illegally abducted and forcefully deported to Turkiye. Under these circumstances, we kept waiting to see if any change of government would bring a positive change in the policies against the PakTurk Schools and the Turkish educators.

Imran Khan, a persistent politician and former cricketer, brought the end of Nawaz Sharif and, supported by the Pakistan Army, also toppled Shehbaz Sharif in the Punjab, the Sharif family's stronghold for decades. During Imran Khan's captaincy, the Pakistan National Cricket Team became the 1992 World Champion for the first time in the country's history, and Khan became a star with his performance and charismatic sportsmanship. After cricket, he founded cancer hospitals in Pakistan. With a foundation and intensive campaigns, he founded Shaukat Khanum Memorial Cancer Hospitals, one in Lahore and one in Peshawar, named after his mother. In these hospitals, 75% of cancer patients are treated for free. Having gained public appreciation for these, Imran Khan entered politics and founded his own party, Pakistan Tehrik-e-Insaaf (PTI), loosely translated as Pakistan Justice Movement, and made an ambitious debut, rising to power through a long struggle and political fights. In 2010, Imran Khan wrote an autobiography where he praised Erdogan for "Democratizing and developing Turkiye and limiting the military's room for maneuver." The ideological vein first determined the political line of Imran Khan was close to political Islam. Therefore, he would get along well with the political Islamist Erdogan.

When Imran Khan was in opposition, his two actions against Turkiye attracted attention. However, he could not sustain his stance. The first was his reaction to targeting PakTurk Schools on the evening of July 15. He posted on Twitter, "What role can Pakistani children play in a coup in a country 5,000 kilometers away?" The second was his decision to boycott the joint parliamentary session at the National Assembly of Pakistan for Erdogan's parliamentary speech, which turned into a show. In both cases, the Turkish Embassy in Islamabad intervened and Imran Khan backed down. In the days that followed, he changed his stance and remained silent and unresponsive to the abduction of the Kaçmaz family and the ensuing lawlessness, despite his party's name promising "justice".

The stance of Imran Khan and his party rightly led us to think that "Even if the PTI comes to power, it will not go against Erdogan's wishes" and "A likely PTI government will continue to fulfill Ankara's wishes". It was not until June 2018, two months after the abduction of the Kaçmaz family, that the Turkish teachers in Pakistan started leaving as they realized the UNHCR would not adequately protect them as the circumstances had become increasingly risky on multiple fronts.

After the forced deportation of the Kaçmaz family, a group of religious communities convened and demanded the resignation of the Federal Minister of Justice for allegedly blaspheming Islam in a televised speech. When their demands were rejected, they blocked the main avenue between Islamabad and Rawalpindi. Shahid Khaqan Abbasi, the interim Prime Minister, failed to manage the process and this helped to dissolve his government.

Elections were called in July 2018. The corruption trials of Nawaz Sharif and his children continued. He and his children would be arrested after the trial. Despite this, the Sharif family said they would remain in Pakistan to prove their innocence. They added they would not evade justice and would follow their case in person. As expected, the court announced its verdict on June 6, 2018 and sentenced Nawaz Sharif to 10 years in prison and a pecuniary fine of 8 million Euros.

The announcement of this decision before the election boosted the rise of Imran Khan and his party. Imran Khan came to power on July 27, 2018 elections. Brought to power by the electorate with great hopes, Imran Khan could naturally not change Pakistan's course and the country kept deteriorating in economy and social development almost daily. Imran Khan and his cabinet, who had the carte blanche from the Pakistan Army, acted as if everything was normal and worked on consolidate their power.

EDUCATORS LEFT PAKISTAN
ONE AFTER ANOTHER

It was later revealed Mr. and Mrs. Murat Ervan, who had been hiding somewhere unknown even to their closest friends, had quietly left Pakistan sometime between September 15, 2017 and July 20, 2018, and regained their freedom.

The Ervan family, like hundreds of Turkish teachers and their families, had been severely affected by the psychological violence and oppression carried out by the authorities of Pakistan and Turkiye, and had tried to hold on to life somewhere they informed no one about fearing their safety. Despite tremendous ordeals, they had overcome the days of hardship by holding on to hope and perseverance. They were only heard from after we learned they had left Pakistan quietly and unnoticed.

When Erdogan and the Turkish Embassy in Islamabad realized they would not have the PakTurk Schools transferred to the Maarif Foundation without the support of Pakistan's top judiciary and the Pakistan Army headquarters, they started to get more closer to these institutions during the Imran Khan government. Although the Turkish Embassy in Islamabad was aware of such a solution during the Nawaz Sharif government, it kept its distance from the judiciary and the military, with whom the Sharif government was in a state of discomfort and conflict. Nevertheless, the Ambassador and the diplomats requested support from the judiciary and the military at every opportunity on this issue. With the advent of Imran Khan to rule, Erdogan had a golden windfall. He had a military-backed Pakistani government in power boasting of its election victory in the wake of a critical judicial ruling against its largest political rival.

SUPREME COURT OF PAKISTAN GOT INVOLVED IN THE PAKTURK CASE

The Turkish Embassy in Islamabad charted a new strategy and took action to ensure the transfer of the PakTurk Schools under the guise of "legal action". Pakistani lawyer M. Suhail Sajid appealed to the Supreme Court of Pakistan through the guidance of the Turkish Embassy Islamabad. He presented to the Court the declaration of the Organization of Islamic Cooperation's October 2016 Foreign Ministers Meeting as 'evidence' and demanded that the Hizmet Movement be declared a so-called 'terrorist' organization in Pakistan. Two days after the filing of this case, the hearings were scheduled within two days. The petition to the Supreme Court of Pakistan and the decision based on the "evidence" had been signal flares of an impending execution decided long ago. As it became clear later on, especially after the official visit of Yavuz Selim Kıran, the erstwhile Turkish Deputy Foreign Minister, to Islamabad in October 2018 with a delegation of the Turkish Maarif Foundation, and his statement "We expect serious developments on FETO within a week", and the frequent visits of several high-level Turkish visitors, including then-Interior Minister Süleyman Soylu and then-Defense Minister Hulusi Akar, who made "a series of offers they would not refuse" to the Pakistani authorities, the atmosphere had been set. The Supreme Court of Pakistan judges "hearing the case", almost without letting the PakTurk counsels speak, set the same tone with lawyer Suhail Sajid who had filed the case and asked the state judicial authorities, "Do you think our relations with our brotherly country Turkiye are a joke? Why can't you resolve the issue of these schools?" and said the issue at hand was so sensitive for the relations between the two countries and must be resolved immediately. The hearing was adjourned to December 28, 2018, pending the decision until the return of the Supreme Court of Pakistan Chief Justice Mian Saqib Nisar, who "would visit Turkiye at the invitation of the Embassy of the Republic of Turkiye in Islamabad as a guest of the President of the Constitutional Court of the Republic of Turkiye, Zühtü Arslan, to attend the Shab-e Aroos ceremonies on December 17 and to make a series of official meetings with Turkish state officials."

The Government of Pakistan lost the compensation lawsuit against Karkey Karadeniz Elektrik power-generation company and was sentenced by the International Center for Settlement of Investment Disputes to pay $1.2 billion to the Turkish company. Pakistan had no way to pay this amount. Prime Minister Imran Khan visited Ankara for talks on this issue and requested Erdogan to recommend the company waive its receivables. Erdogan, meanwhile, had been asking for the transfer of the PakTurk Schools for a long time. Seizing the opportunity, Erdogan reached an agreement with Imran Khan and on November 4, 2019, just two months before the transfer of the PakTurk Schools, Imran Khan announced on his Twitter account that his government had reached an agreement with Ankara and that the Karkey Karadeniz Elektrik had waived its receivables. Pakistan had been waiting for the finalization of this lawsuit which it had kept as a trump card for having the PakTurk Schools transferred. Once the lawsuit was finalized, Government of Pakistan disposed of its card and transferred the schools to the Turkiye Maarif Foundation (TMF) in exchange for a $1.2

billion debt write-off. Meanwhile, this amount was the tip of the iceberg considering the kickbacks awarded to Pakistan for the unlawful seizure of the PakTurk Schools. We do not know how much bribery were handed in total.

Before the hearing, the Chief Justice of the Supreme Court of Pakistan was "specially" invited to Turkiye on the occasion of the December 17 Shab-e-Aroos event in Konya and he also had a private meeting with Erdogan. Ahmet Dönmez, a well-informed journalist who followed the events from the beginning, wrote about this visit with the title "Was the decision to transfer the schools taken at this meeting?"

On December 17, 2018, when the Chief Justice of the Supreme Court of Pakistan was in Turkiye, Turkish Interior Minister Süleyman Soylu arrived on an official visit in Islamabad and met with Prime Minister Imran Khan and State Minister for Interior Affairs Shehryar Khan Afridi. As a parent, Shehryar Khan Afridi was no stranger to the case of the PakTurk Schools and he would boast he had slammed the Nawaz Sharif government for its PakTurk Schools policies, saying "I bashed the Sharif government in the British House of Lords on this issue as well."

As fate would have it, another PakTurk parent, the former Federal Minister of Education, had signed the document that officially established the Turkiye Maarif Foundation in Pakistan, while another parent, State Minister for Internal Affairs, who criticized the Federal Education Minister's party and policies, was among the officials who surrendered the PakTurk Schools to the TMF. This way, we could see in firsthand what "it is not what we say but what we do that matters" meant and how politics could distort personalities.

Imran Khan had invited Erdogan to Pakistan during Soylu's first visit, hoping to break the ice frozen after Imran Khan's boycotting of the joint parliamentary session where Erdogan had spoken in November 2016. The Turkish Embassy Islamabad changed its strategy and focused on the Pakistani judiciary and military. On December 18, 2018, the Chief Justice of the Supreme Court of Pakistan Mian Saqib Nisar visited Turkiye and was well taken care of. On December 20, 2018, Erdogan sent Defense Minister Hulusi Akar to Islamabad to meet the top brass of the Pakistani military.

Ten days after returning from Turkiye, then-Supreme Court Chief Justice Mian Saqib Nisar issued a swift ruling in the PakTurk Schools case, without giving the PakTurk Schools' counsel and officials a proper chance to respond, "in light" of the so-called evidence, declaring the former Turkish management of the schools a so-called 'terrorist' organization and ordering the transfer of the PakTurk Schools to the Turkiye Maarif Foundation.

This decision, which surprised the global public opinion, was met with concern. Supreme Court of Pakistan signed a controversial decision only days before the retirement of the Chief Justice Mian Saqib Nisar. On January 17, 2019, three weeks after deciding on December 28, 2018, Chief Justice Nisar retired. Why would a person, after decades of service for his country, take such a notorious decision that would throw his entire career and past in the trash? What did Erdogan offer him? Perhaps one day we will find out.

While the schools were handed over, Prime Minister Imran Khan remained silent. State Minister of Interior Affairs and PakTurk parent Shehryar Khan Afridi was busy taking security measures for the smooth handover of the PakTurk Schools to the TMF. No doubt, the future generations will condemn politicians who blindly implemented all practices that would go down in history as lawlessness for their political fate and mileage. His children educated by the PakTurk teachers will ask their State Minister father Shehryar Khan Afridi, "Dad, why didn't you do anything when our teachers, whom you trusted us to their care and whom you frequently visited to chat over a cup of tea at every opportunity, were slandered as terrorists? Why did you remain silent about their persecution? Why did you support their oppressors?" What will he say? Isn't this sad?

PEAK CONCERNS: TRANSFER PHASE OF THE PAKTURK SCHOOLS TO THE TURKIYE MAARIF FOUNDATION

The schools were handed over to the Turkiye Maarif Foundation and Erdogan had finally achieved his goal. He was on cloud nine! On February 13, 2019, Erdogan made an exclusive visit to Pakistan. He was to thank Imran Khan and the Pakistani officials. Having given the green light to Imran Khan to visit Turkiye after the transfer of the PakTurk Schools, Erdogan hosted Imran Khan in his palace on January 3-4, 2019. Normally, head of state visits are not in the form of "you come, and I will come", but a gap of at least a year between the two visits and meetings are kept. However, since the recent relations between Turkiye and Pakistan were never realized on an official basis, it was like a rapport between two buddies.

TMF took over the PakTurk Schools. Everyone was worried. During a tense meeting with parents in Islamabad, the Pakistani and Turkish officials of the TMF threatened, "We could have had the schools closed, but we didn't!" This way, they wanted to send a harsh message to the parents: "Shut up, and do not oppose the changes!" As if nothing unusual had happened, they wanted the parents to act normal.

When a parent asked, "You had the PakTurk Schools and the Turkish teachers declared a part of a 'terrorist' organization. Why are you using the same name? Aren't you terrorists, then?" the response from the TMF officials was mind-boggling: "They had their activities as PakTurk. We will put a line between and continue education under the name Pak-Turk." What can we say? Proverbially speaking, the devil looks after his own, or in its Turkish equivalent, "One who steals the minaret has a sheath at hand to cover it quick." This must be a testament to brazenness and shamelessness.

Before taking over the PakTurk Schools, the TMF executives said they would reduce the school fees by 50%, However, after taking over the schools, they only reduced the fees by 25%. Right from the beginning, they showed everyone that they propel themselves with lies.

PakTurk Schools were transformed into Erdogan's political mouthpieces through the TMF. Erdogan, who considers himself as the de-facto leader of the Muslim World and no lesser than a caliph, are propagandized in the usurped schools. Among the first actions of the TMF was to display Erdogan's portraits in the administrative rooms and the foyers as if the schools were the offices of the AKP (Justice and Development Party) in Pakistan. With the Supreme

197

Court decision, Pakistan made a political party from another country the owner of a private chain of schools on its own soil. This way, the Pakistani officials made a historic mistake by placing Pakistani private educational institutions under the command of a government that would be here today and gone tomorrow.

With the departure of the Turkish teachers and the handover of the PakTurk Schools, an epoch concluded. In the new era, several major institutions in Pakistan lost their essence, the judiciary became dismantled, and the rights and freedoms got curtailed. The whole world saw what political games could make people do.

PakTurk Schools, operating as an antidote to extremism in Pakistan, kept achieving one success after another while expanding their 28-school network to serve more students and regions across Pakistan. They had also prepared to crown their services with an international university. Besides, non-governmental organizations like the "Kimse Yok Mu Solidarity and Aid Association" would rush to the rescue and relief of the poor and the needy round the year and in rain or shine across Pakistan. The people across the country greatly appreciated such tokens of kindness and selfless services, which we could render within our humble means. Whenever a disaster struck, people would say "PakTurk Schools and the Kimse Yok Mu will help us!" Whenever they visited our schools, Pakistani colleagues and officials asked if we could open a PakTurk School in their city. They considered it a deficiency not to have a PakTurk School in their cities. Students, where we had no schools, competed with one another to win scholarships in school admission exams and have free-of-cost quality education at PakTurk Schools. Who knows, perhaps the PakTurk Schools were the most meaningful gesture the magnanimous people of Anatolia could give to their Pakistani friends as an homage to those who extended a helping hand from the subcontinent to the people of Anatolia during the Turkish War of Independence. Unfortunately, the Erdogan regime, which abides by no law, feigns ignorance of the truth of human rights, and has adopted oppression as its motto. It keeps harming innocent people through the state apparatus. It has interrupted and smashed the dreams of thousands with every attempt it has made to usurp and bring PakTurk educational institutions to their knees.

Meanwhile, the people of Pakistan, who have never stopped supporting us, have shown that even if PakTurk Schools have become a dream interrupted, they remain as planted seeds of love to sprout thousands of flowers and saplings in hearts. They know the PakTurk Schools will emerge and grow stronger with a fresh opportunity, by God's leave.

CHRONOLOGICAL ORDER OF EVENTS

April 1995 - First PakTurk School, PakTurk Islamabad Boys College opened.

June 2006 - PakTurk Schools were awarded the Sitara-e-Eisaar civil award.

2007 – Purpose-built campuses built in Islamabad and Lahore.

2008 - Purpose-built campuses built in Peshawar and Quetta.

May 4, 2008 - The New York Times featured PakTurk Schools on its front page, stating the education model is a panacea to combat radicalism in the region.

November 22, 2008 - PakTurk Islamabad Boys Campus was inaugurated by the Prime Minister of Pakistan Syed Yousaf Raza Gilani and the Deputy Speaker of the Turkish Grand National Assembly Nevzat Pakdil.

October 12-13, 2010 - During his official visit to Pakistan in the wake of the devastating floods, Erdogan asked the Governor of Sindh province to allocate a school plot to build a PakTurk School in Karachi.

2012- PakTurk Education Foundation signed a protocol with the Government of the Punjab for founding of the International Allama Iqbal University.

May 17, 2012- University of the Punjab, one of Pakistan's oldest universities, awarded Fethullah Gulen an Honorary Ph.D. in Education.

November 21, 2012- Punjab Chief Minister Shehbaz Sharif said, "Turkiye has Fethullah Gulen. This added value has more significance than mineral resources such as oil and gas."

February 14, 2013- Speaker of the Turkish Grand National Assembly Cemil Çiçek and his Pakistani counterpart attended the all-Pakistan Inter-School Mathematics Olympiad Award Ceremony as guests of honor.

March 15, 2013- "Kimse Yok Mu Solidarity and Aid Association" built and inaugurated the $4 million Allama Iqbal Town, distributing free houses to flood affectees.

March 15, 2013 - Multan Boys High School Groundbreaking Ceremony was held with the participation of Punjab provincial government officials and the AKP MPs.

January 2014- The Erdogan regime-backed South Asian Strategic Studies Center (GASAM) started targeting the PakTurk Schools in Pakistan through its publications and reports. Shortly later, the organization intensified its media presence by disseminating articles like "Are You Aware of the Gulen Movement?" in Pakistani media.

February 12, 2014 – Prime Minister of Pakistan Mian Muhammad Nawaz Sharif praised PakTurk Schools at a trilateral summit in Turkiye

April 2014- Construction of the Multan Boys High School halted.

April 2014- The plot allocation protocol for a PakTurk School in Rawalpindi was unilaterally canceled.

April 2014- The protocol for the founding of the International Allama Iqbal University was unilaterally canceled.

January 7, 2016- Federal Minister of Education attended the PakTurk Schools' all-Pakistan Inter School Mathematics Olympiad (ISMO) Award Ceremony as chief guest.

May-June 2016 – The Ministry of Interior Affairs received the visa extension documents of the Turkish teachers working at the PakTurk Schools. The follow-up visits revealed how the officials kept the PakTurk officials in the dark for a long time, always assured them against worries, and stated that the procedure was in progress, whenever they were asked.

May 2016- Capital Development Authority (CDA) officials in Islamabad started harassing visits to the PakTurk Schools and demanded with the threat of punishment consecutive construction reviews that were not imposed upon any other school.

June 2016- Turkiye Maarif Vakfı (Turkiye Maarif Foundation) was founded by Erdogan government.

July 15, 2016- A faux coup was staged in Turkiye.

July 16, 2016- Pakistani social media trolls called for protests in front of the PakTurk campuses.

July 20, 2016- Turkish Embassy in Islamabad ceased processing the official business of the Turkish educators.

July 22, 2016- Ambassador of the Republic of Turkiye to Pakistan Sadık Babür Girgin targeted the PakTurk Schools in a press conference and called for their closure.

August 2, 2016 – Turkish Foreign Minister Mevlüt Çavuşoğlu visited Islamabad and demanded the handover of the PakTurk Schools.

August 9, 2016 - PakTurk PTA issued a press statement and reacted against Mevlüt Çavuşoğlu's statement demanding the closure or handover of the PakTurk Schools.

August 10, 2016 - PakTurk Schools across Pakistan opened their campuses to local and international media organizations for a day after the speculations.

August 10, 2016 – Within the frame of its localization drive, PakTurk Education Foundation appointed Pakistani principals to the PakTurk Schools.

August 25, 2016 – Government of the Punjab appointed four trustees to the management of the PakTurk Education Foundation and forced four Turkish-national board members to resign.

August 26, 2016 – Punjab Chief Minister Shehbaz Sharif attended the inauguration of the Yavuz Sultan Selim Bridge in Istanbul as Erdogan's special guest.

September 9, 2016- The visas of the Turkish educators working at the PakTurk Schools got expired. No visa extensions had been made.

October 17, 2016- The blatant lie that the Organization of Islamic Cooperation (OIC) proscribed the Hizmet Movement as a 'terrorist' organization at the Tashkent Foreign Ministers Summit was circulated by the Turkish government, in Pakistan and worldwide.

November 7-9, 2016 – Presidential Chief Advisor İlnur Çevik visited Pakistan and wrote in a daily column on his return to Turkiye, "The President will be in Pakistan next week and will pull the ears of some for not taking radical steps on the PakTurk issue."

November 15, 2016- Turkish educators working at the PakTurk Schools received an official letter from the Ministry of Interior Affairs, ordering their deportation within three days.

November 16, 2016- Erdogan arrived in Islamabad for an official visit.

November 16, 2016- Following the swift signing of a protocol between the Turkiye Maarif Foundation and the Federal Ministry of Education, the Islamabad office of the TMF was opened.

November 16, 2016- Due to immense backlash, the Pakistani officials verbally informed the PakTurk officials they had extended the deportation deadline until November 30.

November 24, 2016- UNHCR granted asylum seeker certificates to the Turkish educators.

November 29, 2016- Lahore High Court stayed the deportation order. Subsequently, the Sindh and Peshawar High Courts followed.

February 2017- Government of Pakistan's plan to seize the PakTurk Schools through an overnight amendment in the Companies Law instigated by a recommendation from Turkiye was shelved after the scheme had been leaked to the media.

February 17, 2017 – Daily Dawn: 'UNHCR gives Turkish teachers asylum but no jobs'

February 25, 2017- Prime Minister Nawaz Sharif visited Turkiye.

March 2, 2017 –Turkish Chief of General Staff Hulusi Akar arrived in Islamabad and initiated the discussion of having the PakTurk Schools transferred to a Turkish entity.

March 29, 2017- Speaker of the National Assembly of Pakistan visited Turkiye.

May 4, 2017- Erdogan's Kashmir-themed official visit to India admired in Pakistan.

June 2017- Turkish and Pakistani intelligence agencies agreed on the abduction of the Turkish educators.

June 21, 2017 – Pakistani Chief of General Staff visited Turkiye.

July 9, 2017- Turkish intelligence and police officials arrived in Pakistan on a Boeing 777 to carry out an operation and abduct the Turkish educators. Federal Ministry of Interior Affairs and Pakistan's respective civil and military security authorities reacted strongly and deported the Turkish officials.

September 1, 2017 – With the disqualification of Mian Muhammad Nawaz Sharif by the Supreme Court of Pakistan in the first phase of the corruption trial, PML-N's Shahid Khaqan Abbasi replaced him as the Prime Minister.

August 22, 2017 - Karkey Karadeniz Elektrik power generation company's compensation lawsuit against the

Government of Pakistan amounting billions of dollars dropped a bombshell on the country's agenda.

September 2017- Local intelligence operatives started to surveil the Turkish educators' residences.

September 12, 2017- Pakistani Foreign Minister visited Turkiye.

September 16, 2017- Punjab Chief Minister visited Turkiye. The plan to abduct the Turkish educators, especially the Kaçmaz and Ervan families, from Pakistan had probably been discussed during this visit.

September 27, 2017- The Kaçmaz family was hooded and abducted by unidentified operatives in Lahore.

September 28, 2017- The Ervan family narrowly escaped abduction and went into hiding.

September 27, 2017- Lahore High Court ordered the Attorney General of Pakistan to "find and bring the Kaçmaz family by October 6, 2017".

October 3, 2017- Lahore High Court ruled "Murat Ervan and his family cannot be deported from Pakistan."

October 4, 2017- PakTurk School principal Zekeriya Özşahin picked from his home and held under torture for four hours with the claim that "he might be in contact with Murat Ervan and knew where he was."

October 5, 2017- Pakistan's Foreign Minister Khawaja M. Asif averted providing a clear reply to a question about the Kaçmaz family in a talk he attended at a Washington D.C. think tank. He lied that the Turkish teachers' UNHCR asylum seeker certificates had expired on September 30, 2017 and claimed that the Government of Pakistan had no responsibility for the human tragedy incurred.

October 6, 2017- In court, the Attorney General again denied the state involvement in the abduction of the Kaçmaz family and stated the family could not be traced. The judge lashed out at the Attorney General, saying "I order the family to be produced before this Court by October 16, 2017!"

October 11, 2017- The Washington Post headlined "Turkish Family Abducted in Pakistan, Eyes on Intelligence Agencies".

October 14, 2017- Turkish media shared with the world the news that the Kaçmaz family had been brought into Turkiye through a Turkish National Intelligence (MIT) operation.

October 14, 2017- PakTurk's counsel Asma Jahangir made a statement to the press after the deportation of the Kaçmaz family, saying "A third person or element is involved and I know it. We will get to the root of this incident."

October 16, 2017- Lahore High Court demanded an official written statement from the Attorney General of Pakistan following the deportation news.

October 18, 2017- Human Rights Watch shared with the world the news "Remaining Turkish Teachers Are Also at Risk."

December 29, 2017- İhsan Mustafa Yurdakul was appointed as the Ambassador of the Republic of Turkiye in Islamabad, replacing Sadık Babür Girgin.

May 25, 2018- The UN Human Rights Council (OHCHR) ordered the release of the Kaçmaz family, besides urging Pakistan and Turkiye to pay compensation and demanding the prosecution of the officials involved in the abduction.

June 1, 2018- All Turkish educators left Pakistan as security concerns had reached an all-time high.

June 6, 2018- Nawaz Sharif found guilty in corruption cases and sentenced to 10 years in prison.

July 4, 2018- Mesut Kaçmaz was released in Turkiye.

July 20, 2018- The Ervan family's safe exit from Pakistan revealed.

August 18, 2018- Imran Khan became the Prime Minister of Pakistan.

November 4, 2018- Prime Minister Imran Khan tweeted that the $1.2 billion compensation to be paid by Pakistan in the Karkey Karadeniz Elektrik case had been waived through a deal with Ankara.

December 17, 2018- Supreme Court of Pakistan Chief Justice Mian Saqib Nisar went on an official visit to Turkiye.

December 17, 2018- Turkish Minister of Interior Suleyman Soylu arrived in Islamabad on an official visit.

December 20, 2018- Turkish Defense Minister Hulusi Akar arrived in Islamabad on an official visit.

December 28, 2018 — A three-member bench of the Supreme Court of Pakistan signed on the decision to transfer the PakTurk Schools to the Turkiye Maarif Foundation (TMF) claiming that the PakTurk Schools were "linked to a terrorist organization".

December 29, 2018- TMF took over the PakTurk Schools after slandering them as part of a so-called terrorist organization. Continuing without changing the name of the schools, they showed the terrorism slander was always a blatant pretext.

January 2019- Erdogan's photographs are displayed in the foyers and offices of the newly-renamed Pak-Turk Maarif Schools.

January 3-4, 2019 –Prime Minister Imran Khan paid an official visit to Ankara thanks to the green light given to him after the successful handover of the PakTurk Schools.

January 17, 2019 - Chief Justice of the Supreme Court of Pakistan Mian Saqib Nisar retired 20 days after his bench's damning decision on the PakTurk Schools.

February 13, 2019 - Erdogan paid a visit of gratitude to Islamabad for attaining the handover of PakTurk Schools.

April 10, 2022 – Imran Khan become the first Prime Minister of Pakistan in history to be removed from office by a vote of no confidence in the National Assembly of Pakistan.

April 11, 2022 – Mian Muhammad Shehbaz Sharif, former Chief Minister of the Punjab province, became the Prime Minister of Pakistan. As of July 2023, he remains on his post until an interim government assumes power by mid-August until September-October 2023 elections.

AN EXPRESSION OF GRATITUDE

I owe a debt of gratitude to all our Pakistani colleagues, students, graduates, parents, and friends who did not leave us alone, who embraced us in their hearts, and stood upright while supporting us amidst all pressure. I would like to thank Mr. Alamgir Khan, a refined gentleman who beams wisdom through his age, who – as the chief executive of the PakTurk Educational Institutions – never let us feel abandoned and did everything in his power to defend and protect the PakTurk Schools at every phase. I would also like to thank the media in Pakistan for their 20-day uninterrupted coverage of the pressures in the wake of the dastardly coup conspiracy in Turkiye and the lawless practices against the Turkish teachers in Pakistan, especially the Kaçmaz family, and for always defending our rights. I would like to thank every volunteer and human rights defender who organized rallies supporting the Kaçmaz family and the Turkish teachers in various parts of the world from Toronto to London, from New York to Vienna, and from Calgary to Geneva during our hardest times in Pakistan. I would like to thank the 5581 people who supported our campaigns actively on and off the social media. I would like to thank the unsung heroes, our colleagues, who braced the magnitude of the incidents and remained steadfast for the rescue and recovery of the Kaçmaz family despite all hardships, and most importantly, their spouses and children who rooted for them through their invaluable support during the times of hardship. I would like to thank the Journalists and Writers Foundation for its active role throughout the phase of thwarting the deportation of the Kaçmaz family and ensuring their release after their abduction to Turkiye, for its active role in liaising with all national and international institutions and organizations, especially with the United Nations, the UNHCR and the OHCHR, and for its active role in the OHCHR's decision to "free the Kaçmaz family".

INDEX

Karzai, Hamid, 28

Kashmir, 15, 18, 19, 24, 51, 72, 73, 74, 75, 205,

Khan, Alamgir, 67, 68, 69, 70, 71, 82, 83, 210,

Khan, Imran, 42, 50, 59, 60, 107, 146, 186, 187, 188, 189, 191, 193, 194, 195, 196, 208, 209

> boycott   188
>
> filed a case   187
>
> captaincy   181
>
> Shaukat Khanum Memorial Cancer Hospitals 188
>
> backed down   189
>
> visited Ankara   193
>
> praises Erdogan   188
>
> invited Erdogan to Pakistan 195
>
> remained silent   189, 195

Khan, Muhammad Yaqoob, 24, 33

Khan, Nisar Ali, 131,

Khan, Rana Sanaullah, 66, 89, 163,

Khanzada, Shahzeb, 163,

Kimse Yok Mu, 18, 19, 20, 198,

Kundi, Faisal Karim, 17,

L

Lahore Press Club 150, 155

Lahore High Court 101, 102, 104, 119, 141, 148, 149, 150, 152, 159, 160, 161, 162, 167, 204, 206, 207

M

Munyar, Vahap, 64, 113,

O

OIC, 50, 51, 203,